CAMPAIGN 387

ASSAULT ON THE GOTHIC LINE 1944

The Allied Attempted Breakthrough into Northern Italy

PIER PAOLO BATTISTELLI   ILLUSTRATED BY RAMIRO BUJEIRO

Series editor Nikolai Bogdanovic

OSPREY PUBLISHING
Bloomsbury Publishing Plc
Kemp House, Chawley Park, Cumnor Hill, Oxford OX2 9PH, UK
29 Earlsfort Terrace, Dublin 2, Ireland
1385 Broadway, 5th Floor, New York, NY 10018, USA
E-mail: info@ospreypublishing.com
www.ospreypublishing.com

OSPREY is a trademark of Osprey Publishing Ltd

First published in Great Britain in 2023

© Osprey Publishing Ltd, 2023

A catalogue record for this book is available from the British Library.

ISBN: PB 9781472850140; eBook 9781472850133; ePDF 9781472850126;
XML 9781472850157

23 24 25 26 27   10 9 8 7 6 5 4 3 2 1

Maps by Bounford.com
3D BEVs by Paul Kime
Index by Alison Worthington
Typeset by PDQ Digital Media Solutions, Bungay, UK
Printed and bound in India by Replika Press Private Ltd.

Artist's note

Readers may care to note that the original paintings from which the colour
plates in this book were prepared are available for private sale. All
reproduction copyright whatsoever is retained by the publishers. The artist
can be contacted at the following email address:

ramirobujeiro@yahoo.com.ar

The publishers regret that they can enter into no correspondence upon
this matter.

Osprey Publishing supports the Woodland Trust, the UK's leading woodland
conservation charity.

To find out more about our authors and books visit
www.ospreypublishing.com. Here you will find extracts, author
interviews, details of forthcoming events and the option to sign up for
our newsletter.

Author's acknowledgements

The author gratefully acknowledges the help and support provided by
Filippo Cappellano (Rome), Piero Crociani (Rome), Paolo Formiconi
(Lanuvio), Minas Laggaris (Thessaloniki), Lieutenant-Colonel (ret.) Dr
Christopher Pugsley (Wakanae, New Zealand) and Dr Klaus Schmider
(Sandhurst). The author is particularly grateful to the series editor Nikolai
Bogdanovic, and to Marc Romanych of Digital History Archive, whose help
and support proved invaluable.

Dedication

In fond memory of my friend and brother Minas Laggaris.

Abbreviations, acronyms and key terms

AAA	anti-aircraft artillery
AOK	Armee Oberkommando (army)
BR	British
BRZ	Brazilian
CCA	Combat Command A
CCB	Combat Command B
CiC	commander-in-chief
CDN	Canadian
FEB	Força Expedicionária Brasileira (Brazilian Expeditionary Force)
GK	Greek
HQ	headquarters
IND	Indian
IT	Italian
Monte	Mount (Italian for mountain)
NZ	New Zealand
OKH	Oberkommando der Wehrmacht (High Command of the Armed Forces)
PAK	Panzerabwehrkanone (anti-tank gun)
POL	Polish
PPCLI	Princess Patricia Canadian Light Infantry
RCT	Regimental Combat Team
SP	self-propelled
US	United States

Unit designations

Allied units are denoted by their nationality first (e.g. BR, US, CDN etc.)
German units retain their original-language denominations, as per Armee
Oberkommando (army), Korps (corps – Armee, Panzer, Fallschirm, Gebirgs
or generic, armoured, parachute and mountain), and Division – Infanterie
(infantry, subsequently redesignated Grenadier), Panzer (armoured),
Panzergrenadier (mechanized infantry), Fallschirmjäger (paratroop),
Gebirgs (mountain) and Jäger (light infantry).

  Battalions of regiments are referred to using Roman numerals, e.g.
I./363rd RCT (1st Battalion, 363rd Regimental Combat Team). Companies
within regiments are referred to using Arabic numerals or letters, e.g. A./
I./363rd RCT (Company A, 1st Battalion, 363rd Regimental Combat Team).

Front cover main illustration: The battle for Livergnano:
German infantry attack with the support of a self-propelled gun.
(Ramiro Bujeiro)

Title page photograph: A StuG III destroyed by II Polish Corps in
the Gothic Line fighting. (Public Domain)

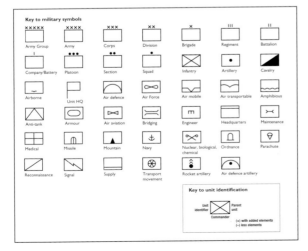

CONTENTS

ORIGINS OF THE CAMPAIGN

The 1944 Gothic Line campaign in Italy is perhaps one of the most debated World War II operations, historians being divided in their opinions as to whether it was a missed strategic opportunity, or just a repetition of the previous campaign that focused on Cassino.

Field Marshal Harold Alexander was the mind behind the Gothic Line campaign, which he advocated as part of a wide-ranging strategic concept. The idea of an offensive through central and northern Italy to reach its eastern borders before advancing into the Balkans dated back to October 1943, although at that point it was conceived merely as a deception. The idea was not discussed until June 1944 when, following the seizure of Rome and the advance into central Italy, Allied commanders began to consider their next steps. There was a basic divergence of opinions about the strategic role of Italy among American and British commanders. The former mostly considered the Mediterranean Theatre as a diversion, the basic purpose of which was to draw reserves away from the Western and Eastern fronts. The British assigned it a fundamental strategic role, and sought to transform the deception into a real plan.

Alexander's concept was to advance through the Gothic Line defences to the Po River and the northern Italian plain with the aim of exploiting the situation either to the north-west (towards France) or to the north-east (into Yugoslavia and Austria). The latter was more attractive; by exploiting the Ljubljana gap (the plain between the Carinthian and Dalmatian mountain ranges), Allied forces could advance along the line Gorizia–Trieste–Ljubljana–Zagreb–Maribor, and from there turn north to drive towards Graz and Vienna. This would cut off German forces in the Balkans and pave the way for an advance into the Reich from the south.

Alexander's plan was rejected by the Combined Chiefs of Staff and by the Allied political leaders, who were themselves debating the actual value of Operation *Dragoon* (initially known as *Anvil*), the landing in southern France. This was the key issue, in spite of the fact that this plan had been approved during the November 1943 Tehran Conference both by Churchill and Roosevelt. Stalin, who preferred an invasion of northern France, was disinclined to agree. Oddly, so was General George C. Marshall, the American Chief of Army Staff, who argued against any distraction from the main theatre of war in the West.

Field Marshal Alexander and US VI Corps commander General John Lucas in discussion at Anzio in early 1944. Alexander was the driving force behind the Allied assault on the Gothic Line. (© Imperial War Museum, NA 12364)

Marshall was not alone in his opinion among the Allied leadership; although General Sir Henry Maitland Wilson, the commander-in-chief (CiC) in the Mediterranean, backed him, Alexander faced opposition from the Chief of Imperial General Staff General Sir Alan Brooke. His opinion on Alexander's idea was that the Allied armies, having reached Ljubljana by September 1944, would become stuck in the area because of the terrain and bad weather. On 2 July 1944, the decision was made to launch the *Dragoon* landings in southern France, and on 7 July, Alexander attended a war cabinet meeting to discuss his plan with Churchill. The British Prime Minister agreed to his proposal and placed at Alexander's disposition the maximum force available. Churchill himself made it clear how vague this promise was by remarking that breaking into the Po valley would have required just half of what had been used for the *Dragoon* plan.

The Gothic Line campaign thus began as a half-hearted solution, albeit with a wide-ranging strategic aim. It did not take long before this was fundamentally altered. In September 1944, as the Allied armies in Italy broke through the Gothic Line defences, the Germans withdrew from Greece and the Yugoslav Partisan leader Josip Tito, following a German attempt on his life, made a secret visit to Moscow to meet with Stalin. Not only did the developing situation alter the strategic concept of Alexander's plan, but the close ties between Tito and the Soviets, who were now advancing into the Balkans, pushed the Gothic Line campaign into a new dimension.

The drive through the Ljubljana gap was no longer seen as a strategic solution, but as an attempt by the British to shape the political configuration of post-war Europe. As such, not only did Tito and the Soviets oppose it, rendering its goals almost impossible, but the situation also created the premises for a long-lasting post-war debate.

By the time of the Second Quebec Conference in mid-September 1944, the Gothic Line campaign had already lost much of its importance. Churchill began considering a landing at Trieste, a plan that was never fully developed. Only Alexander held to the original plan, retaining his aim of an advance into the Balkans, until spring 1945 when the Allied armies eventually broke into the Po valley plain.

Generalfeldmarschall Albert Kesselring studies a map of the strategic situation. To his right is General Richard Heidrich, commander of 1.Fallschirmjäger-Division. (Keystone/Getty Images)

CHRONOLOGY

1944

4 August	The plans for Operation *Olive* are laid down. BR Eighth Army starts regrouping.
15 August	Allied landing in southern France, Operation *Dragoon*.
16–18 August	The orders for Operation *Olive* are issued. BR XIII Corps is placed under the command of US Fifth Army.
25 August	Start of Operation *Olive*. BR Eighth Army attacks the German defensive line on the Metauro River.
1 September	BR Eighth Army breaches the Gothic Line. The Germans begin their withdrawal from Greece.
12–16 September	Second Quebec Conference between Churchill and Roosevelt.
13 September	Start of the US Fifth Army offensive to seize the Apennine mountain passes.
18 September	US Fifth Army takes the Giogo Pass, breaching the Gothic Line.
21 September	BR Eighth Army seizes Rimini.
22 September	US Fifth Army secures the Futa Pass.
26 September	As BR Eighth Army crosses the Marecchia River, breaching the Rimini Line, and US Fifth Army advances beyond the Gothic Line, General Henry Maitland Wilson issues orders to occupy Greece.
30 September	Soldiers from 16.SS-Panzergrenadier-Division massacre all the inhabitants of Marzabotto, which is then destroyed.
12 October	BR 4th Infantry Division and GK 3rd Mountain Brigade are ordered to prepare for transfer to Greece. Athens is seized this same day by British troops.
16 October	BR Eighth Army reaches the Pisciatello River.
20 October	US Fifth Army reaches Monte Grande on the way towards Imola while BR Eighth Army seizes Cesena.
23 October	Feldmarschall Kesselring is injured in a car crash and is replaced by General von Vietinghoff.

24 October	German withdrawal to the Ronco River. US 34th Infantry Division pushes to within 16km of Bologna to Monte Belmonte. General Wilson declares that the offensive cannot be sustained after 15 November.
25–26 October	US II Corps' offensive is halted first, followed by the stop imposed on BR Eighth Army by heavy rain and river flooding.
9 November	BR Eighth Army seizes Forlì and advances towards Faenza.
12 November	Field Marshal Alexander appeals to the Italian partisans to cease fighting during winter.
28 November	Field Marshal Alexander issues orders for the final offensive towards Bologna, to begin on 7 December.
2–5 December	CDN I Corps seizes Ravenna.
12 December	Field Marshal Alexander is appointed Supreme Allied Commander in the Mediterranean, replacing General Wilson.
16 December	BR Eighth Army seizes Faenza. Allied Armies in Italy HQ is renamed 15th Army Group. General Clark takes over from Alexander. Beginning of the German offensive in the Ardennes.
26–31 December	German attack on the Senio River with Italian troops in support (Operation *Wintergewitter*) against US 92nd Infantry Division.
30 December	Field Marshal Alexander halts the offensive, ending the Gothic Line campaign.

1945

4–11 February	US 92nd Infantry Division attacks on the Senio and along the Tyrrhenian coast.
19 February	US 10th Mountain Division and BRZ 1st FEB launch Operation *Encore*, the final attack before the pause induced by winter.

OPPOSING COMMANDERS

ALLIED

Field Marshal Sir Harold Alexander, Earl of Tunis was born in 1891 into the Irish peerage. He was commissioned in 1910 and served in World War I, being wounded at Ypres and earning a Military Cross and a Distinguished Service Order (DSO). After commanding the 4th Guards Brigade and attending the Staff College and the Imperial Defence College, he served in Turkey and Gibraltar. Promoted brigadier in 1935, Alexander was posted to India where he fought local tribesmen until promoted to major-general in 1937, becoming at 46 the youngest general in the British Army. Serving in France as a divisional commander with the British Expeditionary Force in 1940, Alexander distinguished himself at Dunkirk. Placed in command of BR I Corps, in December 1940 he was promoted lieutenant-general. After heading up Southern Command in Britain and being promoted full general in January 1942 (when he was also knighted), Alexander was posted to Burma, emerging untarnished from the retreat before the Japanese. In August 1942, he replaced Claude Auchinleck as Commander-in-Chief Middle East, with Bernard Montgomery under his command. In February 1943, Alexander became commander of Allied 18th Army Group in Tunisia and, being also General Eisenhower's deputy, from July commanded the land forces in the invasion of Sicily and Italy. Appointed Supreme Allied Commander in the Mediterranean Theatre on 12 December 1944, Alexander was also retroactively promoted to field marshal. After handing over command in October 1945, Alexander became Governor General of Canada before joining Churchill's cabinet in 1952 as Minister of Defence. He retired in 1954, and died in 1969.

The BR Eighth Army commander General Sir Oliver Leese (right) talks to the commander of CDN I Corps Lieutenant-General Harry Crerar (left). (Keystone/Hulton Archive/Getty Images)

Field Marshal Sir Henry Maitland 'Jumbo' Wilson was born in 1881. He served in South Africa, Egypt, India and in World War I, being appointed General in Command of the British Forces in Egypt in June 1939. Wilson subsequently led, with little success, the Allied forces in Greece and, with distinction, those fighting in Iraq and Syria. Made head of the Iraq and Persia Command, in February 1943 Wilson was appointed Commander-in-Chief Middle East, eventually succeeding Eisenhower as Supreme Allied Commander in the Mediterranean Theatre in January 1944. In December 1944, Wilson was promoted to field marshal and sent to Washington to head the British Chiefs of Staff Mission. He retired shortly after his return back home in 1947, and died in 1964.

Replacing Montgomery in command of BR Eighth Army in December 1943, **Lieutenant-General Sir Oliver Leese** completed a career path started in September 1942 when he took over command of BR XXX Corps in North Africa. Born in 1894, Leese was commissioned in 1914 and during World War I was wounded three times, mentioned twice in dispatches and won a DSO. After attending the Staff College at Camberley in 1927–28, as a major he served at the War Office before being posted to India. Sent to France in 1940, Leese impressed Montgomery with his performance at Dunkirk. After various training postings in Britain, in 1941 Leese was promoted major-general and given command of BR XXX Corps, soon becoming Montgomery's favourite corps commander. Finding it hard to adapt to the new theatre of operations, in October 1944 Leese was posted to South-East Asia where his performance in Burma eventually led to his dismissal in April 1945. He retired from the army in 1946, and died in 1978.

On 1 October 1944, **General Sir Richard McCreery** replaced Leese as commander of BR Eighth Army. McCreery was born 1898 and commissioned in 1915. Severely wounded during the war and awarded the Military Cross, McCreery attended the Staff College in 1928–29 and was sent to France in 1939, where he took command of BR 2nd Armoured Brigade. After winning a DSO for his action in France, McCreery was promoted major-general and given command of BR 8th Armoured Division, before being sent to Cairo in March 1941 to advise on the use of armoured forces.

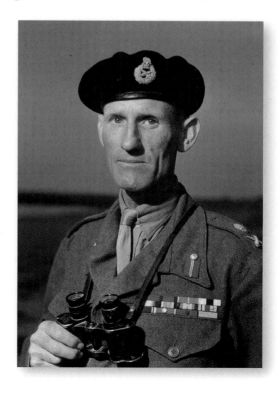

Lieutenant-General Sir Richard McCreery, commander of BR Eighth Army from 1 October 1944. (© Imperial War Museum, TR 2377)

Here, after his dismissal by Auchinleck, he became Alexander's chief of staff. Knighted and promoted lieutenant-general in 1943, McCreery was given command of BR X Corps before the landing at Salerno, and was then given command of BR Eighth Army until 1945. Commander of the occupation forces in Austria, he was promoted to full general in 1948. He retired in 1949, and died in 1967.

As commander of BR V Corps, **General Sir Charles Keightley** was at the forefront of BR Eighth Army during the Gothic Line campaign. Born in 1901 and commissioned in 1921, he served in the Middle East, India and Britain before joining the 1st Armoured Division in France in 1940 as a staff officer. Promoted major-general in 1941, in May 1942 he was given command of BR 6th Armoured Division, which he led during the Tunisian campaign. Promoted lieutenant-general in 1944, that August he was chosen by Leese to take over command of BR V Corps, which he led until 1945. After the war Keightley held various positions including commanding the land forces in the 1956 Suez expedition. He retired from the army in 1958 and was Governor of Gibraltar until 1962. He died in 1974.

Lieutenant-General Eedson L.M. Burns, commander of CDN V Corps, was the prominent non-British Eighth Army commander during the campaign. Born in 1897 near Montreal, he was commissioned in 1915 and served during World War I as a staff officer on the Western Front, where he was wounded twice and awarded a Military Cross. After attending the Imperial Defence College in 1938–39, he went to Britain with CDN 1st Division before becoming Harry Crerar's assistant deputy. Made a temporary brigadier in February 1941, six months later he relinquished the rank and returned to Canada and held backwater posts. Promoted again to temporary brigadier one year later, he was promoted major-general in May 1943 and eventually sent to Italy in January 1944 to exert battle command at the head of CDN 5th Armoured Division. In March 1944, now acting lieutenant-general, he took command of CDN I Corps which he led with distinction, earning a DSO in September. Clashes with other commanders led to his removal on 10 November, Burns being sent to North-West Europe in charge of the CDN First Army rear echelon. After the war, he headed the Department of Veteran Affairs and formed part of the United Nations' peacekeeping mission following the 1948 Arab–Israeli War, and was promoted lieutenant-general in 1958. Burns died in 1985.

General Charles Foulkes replaced Burns as head of CDN I Corps on 10 November 1944. He was born in Britain in 1903 into a poor family, which emigrated to Canada. A provisional lieutenant in 1923, after his commission in 1926 he served in the Permanent Force. A general staff officer from 1934, he had staff training in Britain until 1936 before returning home in 1939. Promoted brigadier in August 1942, Foulkes fought in France at the head of CDN 2nd Division. He was promoted major-general in January 1944, then lieutenant-general in November when he took over CDN I Corps. He served as Chief of the General Staff after the war, and was promoted full general in 1951 when he was appointed Chairman of the Chief of Staff. Foulkes retired in 1960, and died in 1969.

Probably America's most controversial commander, **General Mark Wayne Clark** was born in Madison Barracks, New York, in 1896. Commissioned in 1917, he was wounded while serving in France in 1918. After the war, he served in various staff and training roles, which earned him the reputation of a good trainer of men. Promoted brigadier-general in 1941, in January the following year Clark was appointed Deputy Chief of Staff of the Army Ground Forces, rising to Chief of Staff in May. In April 1942, Clark was promoted major-general, becoming the youngest general in the US Army. Sent to Britain two months later as commander of US II Corps, he worked with General Eisenhower on the feasibility of an Allied landing in Europe. In October, as Eisenhower's deputy, Clark was assigned to the Mediterranean Theatre, where he relinquished command of US II Corps, and was promoted to lieutenant-general in November 1942. Given command of the newly created US Fifth Army in January 1943, Clark had his baptism of fire in September during the Salerno landings, the first of a series of battles US Fifth Army fought in Italy under his command. Often resented for his rapid career progress, which many attributed to his friendships with Eisenhower and Marshall, Clark was criticized for his handling of crucial battles such as Cassino, Anzio and the May 1944 breakthrough to Rome. Critical of the *Dragoon* plan, Clark led US Fifth Army during the Gothic Line campaign until, on 16 December 1944, he replaced Alexander as Supreme Allied

Commander in Italy as CiC of the now renamed 15th Army Group. Promoted full general in March 1945, after the Allied victory Clark commanded US Forces in Austria before serving as deputy to the Secretary of State. In 1952, Clark led the United Nations Forces in Korea, a position he held until 1953, when he retired. He served as president of The Citadel military college in Charleston, South Carolina, until 1965, and died in 1984.

General Lucian K. Truscott, Jr took command of US Fifth Army in December 1944. Born in Chatfield, Texas in 1895, Truscott enlisted in 1917, and received officer training and a commission in October that same year. During the war he remained in the United States, serving in both cavalry and staff assignments until promoted brigadier-general in June 1942. Assigned to Lord Mountbatten's Combined Staff, Truscott returned to the United States where in November 1942 he was promoted major-general, taking part in the Operation *Torch* landings. Given command of US 3rd Infantry Division in March 1943 – one of America's youngest divisional commanders – Truscott fought in Sicily and at Salerno and Anzio before being given command of US VI Corps in February 1944. Following the landings in southern France, in September 1944 Truscott was given command of US Fifteenth Army, an administrative command, until taking over as head of US Fifth Army from Clark. He led US Third Army from October 1945, and retired from the army in 1947. From 1951, Truscott worked as an adviser to the CIA, until his retirement in 1958. He died in 1965.

Major-General Geoffrey Keyes commanded US II Corps, which spearheaded US Fifth Army's offensive against the Gothic Line. He was born in 1888 at Fort Bayard, New Mexico. Commissioned in 1913, Keyes fought in Mexico and was a language instructor at West Point before being posted to Panama after World War I. A brigadier-general by 1942, that same year Keyes was promoted major-general and given command of US 9th Armoured Division. He took part in the *Torch* landings and the Sicilian campaign as

Patton's deputy. In September 1943, Keyes took command of US II Corps, a position he held until the end of the war. He then led the US Seventh and Third armies until his retirement in 1950. He died in 1967.

The US IV Corps was commanded by **Lieutenant-General Willis Dale Crittenberger.** He was born in 1890 in Baltimore, Maryland, and commissioned in 1913. After attending the General Staff College at Fort Leavenworth and the United States Army War College in Washington, Crittenberger served as a cavalry staff officer until appointed chief of staff of US 1st Armored Division, which he commanded from February 1942, following his promotion to brigadier-general. In August, following his promotion to major-general, he was given command of US III Armored Corps. Redesignated US XIX Corps, it relocated to Britain in January 1944. Crittenberger took command of US IV Corps in Italy in March 1944. Deployed at the front from June 1944, he led this corps until the end of the war. Promoted (temporary) lieutenant-general in June 1946, after the war Crittenberger held several commands until his retirement in 1952, which was followed by a period as adviser to President Eisenhower. He died in 1980.

AXIS

Generalfeldmarschall Albert Kesselring is the German commander most closely associated with the Italian campaign. Born in 1893 in Bayreuth, after his commission in 1906 he served during World War I as an aide to various Bavarian artillery commanders before being promoted captain and serving as staff officer at divisional and corps level. After the war he joined the Reichswehr, serving in the training department of the War Ministry. In October 1934, Kesselring was promoted to *Oberst* and joined the newly formed Luftwaffe, for which he received the brevet of pilot. Appointed chief of the Luftwaffe Defence Department, in 1936 he was promoted to *Generalleutnant* and appointed as Luftwaffe Chief of Staff. Promoted to *General der Flieger* in 1937, the following year Kesselring was given command of Luftflotte 1, which he led during the 1939 Polish campaign, earning the Knight's Cross. He took command of Luftflotte 2 in January 1940, and fought in the West and in the Battle of Britain, being promoted to *Generalfeldmarschall* in July that year. After a brief period on the Eastern Front, in December 1941 Kesselring was appointed Oberbefehlshaber Süd (CiC South) for Luftwaffe units in the Mediterranean, and commanded ground units during the campaign in North Africa. In November 1943, Hitler chose Kesselring instead of Rommel to take over command in Italy, from whence he was in charge of German forces in this theatre until his appointment as Oberbefehlshaber West on 11 March 1945. In 1947, Kesselring faced trial for his involvement in the Ardeatine caves massacre in Rome. The death sentence he received was commuted to life imprisonment – from which he was released in 1952. Still a controversial figure, he died in 1960.

On 23 October 1944, Kesselring's car collided with a towed gun. Invalided until 15 January 1945, Kesselring was replaced by **Generaloberst Heinrich von Vietinghoff-Scheel.** The latter was born in 1887 and commissioned in 1907. During World War I, von Vietinghoff earned the Iron Cross and promotion to *Hauptmann* before joining the Reichswehr. Between 1920 and

Generalfeldmarschall Kesselring (second from right), commander of Heeresgruppe C in Italy, in discussion with General Heinrich von Vietinghoff (far left), commander of AOK 10 and his temporary successor. (Narodowe Archiwum Cyfrowe, Public Domain)

1924, he served in various staff positions, joining the War Ministry in 1929. After commanding an infantry battalion in 1931, in 1933 he was promoted to *Oberst*, and two years later was given command of the newly formed 1.Schützen-Brigade. Promoted to *Generalmajor* in 1936, he served with the Wehrmacht's Inspectorate of Armoured and Motorized Troops until 1938, when he was appointed to command 5.Panzer-Division. Having fought in Poland, he commanded XIII.Armee-Korps during the 1940 French campaign. Promoted to *General der Panzertruppe* in 1940 and awarded the Knight's Cross, in November 1940 he took command of XXXXVI.Armee-Korps, which he led in the Balkans and on the Eastern Front. In December 1942, von Vietinghoff took command of AOK 15 in France, and, having been moved to the reserve for health reasons, on 15 August 1943 he was appointed to lead AOK 10 in Italy. After Kesselring's return, von Vietinghoff became commander of Heeresgruppe Kurland before returning to Italy in March 1945, replacing Kesselring once again. He oversaw the surrender of German forces in Italy the following month. Von Vietinghoff died in 1952.

General Joachim Lemelsen was the commander of AOK 14 until he replaced General von Vietinghoff in command of AOK 10 in November 1944. (Narodowe Archiwum Cyfrowe, Public Domain)

General der Panzertruppe Joachim Lemelsen commanded AOK 10. Born in 1888 in Berlin and commissioned in 1908, he served in World War I as an artillery officer, joining the Reichswehr at its conclusion. After holding several commands, in 1935 Lemelsen served at the War School in Dresden. Promoted to *Generalmajor* in 1937, the following year he became commander of 29.Infanterie-Division. He fought in Poland (which earned him promotion to *Generalleutnant*) and France. In May 1940, Lemelsen was made commander of 5.Panzer-Division, and that August was promoted to *General der Artillerie* (later changed to *General der Panzertruppe*) and was given command of XXXXVII.Armee-Korps on the Eastern Front. In September 1943, after being awarded the Oak Leaves to the Knight's Cross,

General Traugott Herr was commander of LXXVI.Panzer-Korps from June 1943 to November 1944, when he took command of AOK 14. (GHWK – Haus der Wannsee-Konferenz Gedenk- und Bildungsstätte, CC BY 4.0)

he was sent to command LXXXVII.Armee-Korps in Italy. He led AOK 14 from June 1944, and that October replaced von Vietinghoff as head of AOK 10 before returning to AOK 14 in February 1945. Lemelsen died in 1954.

Lemelsen's replacement at AOK 14 was **General der Panzertruppe Traugott Herr**, who until then had led LXXVI.Panzer-Korps. Born in 1890 and commissioned in 1912, Herr was severely wounded during World War I, after which he joined the Reichswehr. He headed a motorized infantry regiment in 1939–40, and in October 1941 was awarded the Knight's Cross. He commanded the 13.Panzer-Division, and was promoted to *Generalmajor* in April 1942. Wounded again in October, in December 1942 he was promoted to *Generalleutnant*. In June 1943 Herr took command of LXXVI.Panzer-Korps, and fought in Italy from then on. Appointed to command AOK 14 on 24 November 1944, on 15 February 1945 he took over AOK 10, replacing Lemelsen. He died in 1976.

General der Artillerie Heinz Ziegler was born 1894 and commissioned in 1914. He fought in World War I, after which he joined the Reichswehr, eventually becoming, in 1939, Commander of the Reserve Army. Promoted to *Generalmajor* in January 1942, he fought in North Africa and, after various staff positions, took command of AOK 14 in October 1944. He relinquished this command on 22 November that same year, and retired from active duty. Ziegler died in 1972.

Two corps commanders are worthy of mention. **General der Panzertruppe Fridolin von Senger und Etterlin**, born 1891 and commissioned in 1914, was promoted to *Generalmajor* in September 1941. The commander of 17.Panzer-Division from October 1942, he fought on the Eastern Front, and was promoted to *Generalleutnant* in May 1943. Sent to Sicily in June 1943, he fought in Italy, taking command of XIV.Panzer-Korps in October and holding this until the surrender. Von Senger died in 1963. **General der Fallschirmtruppe Alfred Schlemm**, born in 1894 and commissioned in 1914, was an artillery officer who fought in World War I and served in the Reichswehr before joining the Luftwaffe in 1938. A staff officer promoted to *Generalmajor* in 1940, in 1942 he took command of a temporary unit on the Eastern Front, being promoted to *Generalleutnant* in June and given command of 1.Flieger Division. Thereafter, he commanded II.Luftwaffen-Feld-Korps, before being promoted in January 1943 to *General der Flieger* (later *General der Fallschirmtruppe*). The corps' entire staff was sent to Italy and the unit renamed I.Fallschirm-Korps. After relinquishing command in November 1944 to General Heidrich, Schlemm was given command of 1.Fallschirm-Armee, and was wounded in March 1945. He died in 1986.

OPPOSING FORCES

ALLIED

In August 1944, the Allied armies in Italy were 1.5 million strong with 20 divisions, five of which were armoured. Although an impressive force, it suffered from several weaknesses. The *Dragoon* operation, which took three American and four French divisions from the Italian theatre in July, affected US Fifth Army and its capabilities. In September, it was left with four American infantry and one armoured division, along with one South African division and BR XIII Corps. However, given the different standards and practices in use by the British and the American armies, it was impossible to interchange these units in the same area, which reduced US Fifth Army's actual fighting power.

The four American infantry divisions were given the task of breaking through the Gothic Line, while, to the east, US IV Corps was deployed along the Arno River covering 100km with the South African armoured division and Task Force (TF) 45. The latter was formed on 26 July 1944 from the 45th

A column of infantrymen from British Eighth Army advances along an entrenched pathway on the Gothic Line defences during Operation *Olive* in September 1944. (BIPPA/ Keystone/Hulton Archive/ Getty Images)

Soldiers of the 1st Division of the Força Expedicionária Brasileira (FEB) arriving in Italy, July 1944. (European/FPG/Archive Photos/Getty Images)

Anti-Aircraft Artillery (AAA) Brigade in order to relieve US 34th Infantry Division. Initially made up of the 91st and 107th AAA groups, retrained for use as infantry, the task force had the 2nd Armored Group attached as well as further units (including British and Italian) over time. This impromptu solution was also made necessary by the simultaneous reorganization of US 1st Armored Division, and ended with the division being reduced to two-thirds of its original strength.

The BR XIII Corps, comprising one British infantry, one armoured and one Indian division, was deployed east of Florence, with a separate mission. This corps, plus several newly arrived divisions, increased US Fifth Army's strength from 170,357 on 16 August 1944 to 331,483 on 15 December 1944 (having peaked at 379,588 on 4 June 1944); it would shrink again to 266,513 on 31 March 1945 following the departure of the British units. It is worth noting that American troop strength remained pretty much the same in spite of replacements and reinforcements: 147,014 in August 1944 (having stood at 231,306 on 4 June 1944), 144,476 in December 1944, and 176,392 in March 1945.

This reveals both how hard US Fifth Army fought in the Apennines, and also its weaknesses. The brunt of the fighting fell, almost entirely, on the infantry, particularly at battalion and company level. Although most of the US infantry division's strength (some 14,000) derived from its three infantry regiments (each 3,200 strong), the number of infantrymen actually fighting was quite limited, and losses hit them hardest. This required each division to have a period of rest and recovery before returning to the front, but, since there were no reserves, US Fifth Army was unable to sustain a high tempo in its offensives.

Even though the number of American replacements sent to US Fifth Army exceeded the losses incurred (19,997 men between 15 August and 15 December 1944, 18,958 between 16 December 1944 and 31 March 1945), the effects of this intake became manifest only in February and March 1945. By then, the American divisions had been reorganized, each with 4,500 men above established strength. Also, since losses particularly affected officers and NCOs, necessitating promotion from the ranks, in February 1945 US Fifth Army created an officer cadet school. By then, US Fifth Army was fully capable of carrying out a major offensive.

It is worth noting that US Fifth Army was the only army to receive reinforcements. The 6th Regiment of the 1a Divisão de Infantaria Expedicionária, the army component of the Brazilian Força Expedicionária Brasileira (1st FEB), arrived in Italy in July 1944, and was subsequently deployed to the US IV Corps sector in mid-September. The division, which conformed to American Tables of Organization and Establishment (TOEs), arrived in Italy lacking adequate weapons and training, which greatly delayed its deployment to the front and its effectiveness. The 1st and 11th regiments, which arrived in October 1944, brought the total strength, on 15 December that year, to 13,000 (increasing to 14,230 on 15 March 1945), but the division was not fully operational until 1945.

African-American soldiers also served in Anti-Aircraft Artillery units, part of which would form US TF 45. These men from US 92nd Infantry Division are setting up a Bofors 40mm AA gun. (Galerie Bilderwelt/ Getty Images)

The US 92nd 'Buffalo' Infantry Division, made up of African-American soldiers, only included 2 per cent of all the African-American soldiers in the US Army. Recruitment of African-American soldiers began with the 16 September 1940 Selective Service Act. However, US 92nd Division, which had been formed in 1917 and fought in World War I, was reactivated at Fort McClellan, Alabama on 15 October 1942. Its 370th Regimental Combat Team (RCT) arrived in Italy at the end of August and, after being attached to the 1st Armored Division, formed TF 92. Following the arrival of the rest of the division in October–November, the 92nd was deployed to relieve TF 45, and suffered in the December 1944 German counter-attack. The division's poor early performance was attributed to inadequate leadership and training, with the result that it was reorganized in March and April 1945. Among the 92nd's units were the African-American 366th Infantry Regiment, the 473rd RCT and the Nisei 442nd InfantryRegiment.

Well trained and well equipped, US 10th Mountain Division was activated at Camp Hale, Colorado on 15 July 1942. Its 86th Mountain Regiment first arrived in Italy on 22 December 1944. The division was deployed to the front in January 1945, and soon distinguished itself in the February–March offensives that concluded the Gothic Line campaign.

With a total of 11 divisions BR Eighth Army was a truly cosmopolitan force, with British (three infantry, one armoured), New Zealand (one infantry), Indian (two infantry), Canadian (one infantry, one armoured) and Polish (two infantry) divisions. Still, they were perfectly integrated thanks to the common standards and practices learnt by British, Commonwealth and Imperial troops during troop and staff training. Armour and firepower were its main strengths; on the eve of the start of the offensive, BR Eighth Army deployed 1,089 Sherman and 187 Churchill tanks, plus 287 light Stuarts, along with 1,055 anti-tank (149 of which were M10 self-propelled) and 1,222 artillery guns.

A group of infantrymen from the US 10th Mountain Division fires at the enemy. The man on the left still has the cover on his M1 Garand rifle muzzle. (US Army)

Lance-Corporal Sawaran Singh, a military policeman with the IND 8th Division, directing traffic in Italy. The often neglected contribution of the Indian Army to the Italian campaign was substantial. (PhotoQuest/Getty Images)

BR Eighth Army's weakness was its shortage of infantry. Even though in August 1944, 64 of its 71 infantry battalions were at full strength, the British Army estimated that within a month there would be a deficit of 21,000 soldiers in its units alone. The infantry situation was already critical, and steps had been taken. In July, the Canadians decided to convert AAA and reconnaissance units into infantry, forming the 12th Canadian Infantry Brigade, including the Lanark & Renfrew Scots Regiment (formerly an AAA unit), the motorized Westminster Regiment and the 4th Princess Louise's Dragoon Guards (a reconnaissance unit). Even though CDN I Corps could rely on the manpower pool of its relatively large support units, eventually it had to resort to using light forces to deal with the shortage of replacements.

This shortage was particularly acute for the Polish Corps; it was missing one infantry brigade, and made good the losses suffered at Cassino with 4,000 men taken from service and HQ units. Likewise, the 2nd New Zealand Division was missing one infantry brigade, and only the Indian divisions, relying on an efficient replacement system linked directly to India, were able to maintain their infantry battalions at an average strength of 800 men each.

The British Army suffered the most, for various reasons. The conversion of AAA troops into infantry units began in June with a first batch of 3,400 men, followed by 5,000 in July, 2,000 in August and 6,600 in September, for a rough total of 17,000. Since practically no replacements were sent to Italy, British units soon faced a serious shortage of infantry, caused by losses and desertions. This highlighted the British Army's manpower crisis, made clear by front-line infantry units' increasing overall losses as the offensive progressed. A total of 628 deserters in August increased to 944 in September, falling to 905 in October, before rising again to 1,200 in November, 1,211 in December and 1,127 in January 1945. Some infantry divisions were particularly affected, notably the BR 46th (1,059 desertions between August and December), BR 56th (990 in the same period) and BR 78th (927 between October and December). It was soon clear that measures were needed to reduce the number of desertions.

On 22 September, Alexander accepted his staff's proposal to reduce the number of rifle companies from four to three in each infantry battalion, reducing their strength from 845 to 730. Furthermore, BR 1st Armoured Division was broken up and practically disbanded, its BR 18th Infantry Brigade being reduced to cadre and its BR 2nd Armoured Brigade turned into an independent unit. The BR 56th Infantry Division was spared the same fate, because the South Africans provided a second infantry brigade for the Armoured Division, freeing up BR 24th Guards Brigade. Nevertheless, BR 168th Brigade from BR 56th Division was also reduced to cadre, and replaced by BR 43rd Gurkha Lorried Infantry Brigade to add manpower to BR 56th Division.

A last factor was the unexpected shortage of artillery ammunition afflicting BR Eighth Army in the later stages of the offensive, due to mistaken calculations and insufficient supply. This was at a time when US Fifth Army was able to fire an average of 12,000 rounds per day during the offensive, and even the Germans could reply with an average of 400–500. This was the final straw in the decision to transfer units from Italy. Between October 1944 and January 1945, one British and one Indian division were sent to Greece (along with GK 3rd Mountain Brigade), a country by then facing civil war. BR Eighth Army was reduced in size in March 1945 when CDN I Corps and one British infantry brigade were transferred to the Western Front, heralding the end of the Gothic Line campaign.

AXIS

The idea of a fortified position running along the Italian northern Apennines originated with Generalfeldmarschall Erwin Rommel who, as commander of Heeresgruppe B in northern Italy, outlined it to Hitler. Rommel's strategy envisaged a withdrawal from southern and central Italy in order to gain time and build the line, which, exploiting the natural barrier of the Apennine

Mussolini inspecting troops of the 4th Mountain Division 'Monte Rosa' training in Germany, in mid-1944. Four Italian divisions would be deployed on the Gothic Line. The Monte Rosa arrived at the front in late October, and fought against the Força Expedicionária Brasileira in the Serchio area. (ullstein bild via Getty Images)

A Waffen-SS soldier receiving orders by field telephone in northern Italy. The only Waffen-SS unit in Italy was 16.SS-Panzergrenadier-Division 'Reichsführer-SS', which earned a sinister reputation for crimes committed against civilians. (ullstein bild via Getty Images)

An Organisation Todt (OT) propaganda poster exhorting Italian workers to donate their labour to construction projects in Italy. The initial construction work of the Gothic Line fortifications was undertaken by the OT. (Public Domain)

mountain range, would enable it to halt the Allied advance. The Apennin Stellung (Apennine Position) was to be the last line of defence in Italy before the Alps and the German border. Taking command in Italy in November 1943, Kesselring maintained the idea of the last line of defence, but focused on defending the positions in central Italy for as long as possible.

Unsurprisingly, the development of the Apennin Stellung, renamed the Goten Linie (Gothic Line) in May 1944, proceeded at a slow pace, given the changes in command in the area where it was to be built: AOK 14 (from November 1943) and Armee Gruppe von Zangen (from February 1944). Reconnaissance for the building of fortified positions began in September 1943, with construction commencing two months later, until in February 1944 two engineer commands took over the whole project. It was soon clear that manpower resources, mostly provided by Organisation Todt using Italian workers, were insufficient and inadequate. Yet by March 1944, some 400 fortified fighting positions had been built, mostly in the mountainous eastern area. On 2 June, Hitler ordered an acceleration in the construction of the Gothic Line, focusing on the western area, where the terrain was less suitable for defence.

On 15 June, the Gothic Line was officially renamed the Grüne Linie (Green Line), and on 5 July, the withdrawing AOK 10 and AOK 14 took over the construction of its fortifications. It was soon clear that the Gothic, or Green, Line had many weaknesses. Mistakes were made from the outset, when its future defensive positions were located using reconnaissance from the south. As a result, the various positions, or strongpoints, were not connected to each other, especially in the mountainous areas where troops were required to move downhill and up again to shift from one position to another. Another issue was the shortage of shelters for artillery. It also became clear that the defensive positions mostly focused on the areas best suited for defence, resulting in the less suitable ones remaining undefended.

The major issue was the lack of depth in the line. Only in a few places did strongpoints stretch back to cover a relatively large area, but behind them there was nothing. As a result, on 5 July, Kesselring ordered a reconnoitring of the area in order to construct a second defensive line running between 15 and 40km behind the Grüne Linie. What was to be known as Grüne (Green) II was in fact a series of strongpoints which did not form an actual defensive line. The same applied to the subsequent defensive lines developed by the Germans, which in many cases were only present on maps.

A closer look at the Gothic Line defences in the AOK 10 area in August 1944 shows that they mostly consisted of earthworks, offering little chance of prolonged resistance. AOK 10 reported the availability of only ten strongpoints plus two under construction, with 2,375 machine-gun nests plus 272 others still under construction. However, only 16 machine-gun nests were fortified, and only four of the famous 'Panther turret' positions had been completed, with 18 more on the way. Mines were also scarce, with just 72,000 anti-tank T-mines being laid, along with 23,000 anti-personnel S-mines.

German resistance eventually owed more to the availability of forces rather than the use of defensive positions. It is worth noting that, in spite of misconceptions, the Italian front had not been strengthened since the summer of 1944. On 15 August, Heeresgruppe C had a total of 27 divisions under its command, rising to 30 one month later. The breakdown included one Panzer division and only three Panzergrenadier divisions, two having been transferred to the Western Front. The actual increase was down to two second-rate infantry divisions withdrawing from France to Italy, to the transfer of one division from the Balkans and the arrival in Italy of two Italian divisions trained in Germany and rated fit for anti-partisan duties only. Throughout the Gothic Line campaign until December 1944, Heeresgruppe C had between 29 and 30 divisions which, other than the single Panzer and the three Panzergrenadier ones, included two Fallschirmjäger divisions and two to four Italian ones, its infantry divisions shrinking from 22 to 19.

Available data show that the total strength of Heeresgruppe C's divisions remained more or less at the same level, rising from 258,721 on 1 July (96,288 of whom were combat effective) to 273,697 (of whom 109,887 were combat effective) on 1 November 1944, with basically the same divisions. These figures also show that replacements were regularly sent to Italy, which enabled the divisions to remain up to strength, in spite of losses. The same applied to armoured vehicles and anti-tank guns.

In late July, Heeresgruppe C reported the availability of 263 tanks (136 of which were serviceable; the figures include 56 PzKpfw III tanks all deployed on the north-eastern border), 192 (83 serviceable) Sturmgeschütz, 167 (96 serviceable) Italian self-propelled (SP) guns and 498 (466 serviceable) PAK guns. The 118 PzKpfw IV tanks rose to 166 in November before shrinking to 117 in December, while PzKpfw V 'Panther' numbers fell from 39 in November to 32 in December 1944. Available Tiger tanks shrank from 60 in July to 36 in November and December. Sturmgeschütz numbers increased to 191 in November and to 251 in December, while Italian SP gun numbers decreased to 148 in December. PAK gun numbers also increased to 507 in December.

On 20 August, AOK 10 reported the availability of 81 infantry battalions, of which only 23 were at strength (containing 400 men or more), with the remaining 23 at medium strength, 26 at average strength (fewer than 300 men) and nine rated as weak (200 men or fewer). AOK 10 also had 51 Sturmgeschütz, 164 PAK and 351 field artillery guns, numbers that paled in comparison to those in BR Eighth Army. However, the Germans managed their reserves well and were able to keep their units up to strength.

A Turcoman soldier training on a rubber boat. The 162.Infanterie-Division was largely composed of either volunteers or drafted POWs from Turkmenistan. (ullstein bild via Getty Images)

ORDERS OF BATTLE, 25 AUGUST 1944

ALLIED

Supreme Allied Commander, Mediterranean Theatre (General Sir Henry Maitland Wilson)
Allied Armies in Italy (Field Marshal Sir Harold Alexander)

BR EIGHTH ARMY

(Lieutenant-General Sir Oliver Leese, from 1 October 1944 Lieutenant-General Sir Richard McCreery)

Army reserves
NZ 2nd Infantry Division (Lieutenant-General Sir Bernard Freyberg VC)
    NZ 4th Armoured Brigade
    NZ 5th Infantry Brigade
    NZ 6th Infantry Brigade
GK 3rd Mountain Brigade

BR V Corps (Lieutenant-General Charles F. Keightley)
BR 1st Armoured Division (Major-General Richard A. Hull) (broken up in November 1944, disbanded 1945)
    BR 2nd Armoured Brigade
    BR 18th Infantry Brigade
    BR 43rd Gurkha Lorried Infantry Brigade
BR 4th Infantry Division (Major-General Alfred D. Ward)
    BR 10th Infantry Brigade
    BR 12th Infantry Brigade
    BR 28th Infantry Brigade
BR 46th Infantry Division (Major-General John L.I. Hawkesworth)
    BR 128th Infantry Brigade
    BR 138th Infantry Brigade
    BR 139th Infantry Brigade
    BR 25th Tank Brigade
BR 56th Infantry Division (Major-General John Y. Whitfield)
    BR 167th Infantry Brigade
    BR 168th Infantry Brigade
    BR 169th Infantry Brigade
    BR 7th Armoured Brigade
IND 4th Indian Infantry Division (Major-General Arthur Holworthy)
    IND 5th Infantry Brigade
    IND 7th Infantry Brigade
    IND 11th Infantry Brigade

BR X Corps (Lieutenant-General Sir Richard McCreery)
IND 10th Infantry Division (Major-General Denys W. Reid)
    IND 10th Infantry Brigade
    IND 20th Infantry Brigade
    IND 25th Infantry Brigade
BR 9th Armoured Brigade Group

CDN I Corps (Lieutenant-General Eedson L.M. Burns)
CDN 5th Armoured Division (Major-General Bertram M. Hoffmeister)
    CDN 5th Armoured Brigade
    CDN 11th Infantry Brigade
    CDN 12th Infantry Brigade
CDN 1st Infantry Division (Major-General Christopher Vokes)
    CDN 1st Infantry Brigade
    CDN 2nd Infantry Brigade
    CDN 3rd Infantry Brigade
BR 21st Tank Brigade

POL II Corps (Lieutenant-General Władysław Anders)
POL 3rd Carpathian Infantry Division (Major-General Bronisław Duch)
    POL 1st Carpathian Rifle Brigade
    POL 2nd Carpathian Rifle Brigade
POL 5th Kresowa Infantry Division (Major-General Nikodem Sulik-Sarnowski)
    POL 5th Wilenska Infantry Brigade
    POL 6th Lwowska Infantry Brigade

US FIFTH ARMY

(Lieutenant-General Mark W. Clark)
US II Corps (Major-General Geoffrey T. Keyes)
US 34th Infantry Division (Major-General Charles L. Bolté)
    US 133rd Infantry Regiment
    US 135th Infantry Regiment
    US 168th Infantry Regiment
US 85th Infantry Division (Major-General John B. Coulter)
    US 337th Infantry Regiment
    US 338th Infantry Regiment
    US 339th Infantry Regiment
US 88th Infantry Division (Major-General Paul W. Kendall)
    US 349th Infantry Regiment
    US 350th Infantry Regiment
    US 351st Infantry Regiment
US 91st Infantry Division (Major-General William G. Livesay)
    US 361st Infantry Regiment
    US 362nd Infantry Regiment
    US 363rd Infantry Regiment

US IV Corps (Lieutenant-General Willis D. Crittenberger)
US 1st Armored Division (Major-General Vernon E. Pritchard)
    US Combat Command A
    US Combat Command B
    Attached: US 370th Regimental Combat Team, US 92nd Infantry Division (forming TF 92)
SA 6th Armoured Division (Major-General William H.E. Poole)
    SA 11th Armoured Brigade
    SA 12th Motorized Brigade
    Attached: BR 24th Guards Brigade
US Task Force 45 (Brigadier-General Cecil L. Rutledge)

BR XIII Corps (Lieutenant-General Sidney C. Kirkman)
BR 6th Armoured Division (Major-General Horatius Murray)
    BR 26th Armoured Brigade
    BR 1st Guards Brigade
    BR 61st Infantry Brigade
BR 1st Infantry Division (Major-General Charles F. Loewen)
    BR 2nd Infantry Brigade
    BR 3rd Infantry Brigade
    BR 66th Infantry Brigade
IND 8th Infantry Division (Major-General Dudley Russell)
    IND 17th Infantry Brigade
    IND 19th Infantry Brigade
    IND 21st Infantry Brigade
CDN 1st Armoured Brigade

AXIS

Heeresgruppe Süd (Generalfeldmarschall Albert Kesselring, from 23 October 1944 Generaloberst Heinrich von Vietinghoff)[1]

AOK 10

(Generaloberst Heinrich von Vietinghoff, from 23 October 1944 General der Panzertruppe Joachim Lemelsen)
LI.Gebirgs-Armee-Korps (General der Gebirgstruppe Valentin Feuerstein)
715.Infanterie-Division (Generalmajor Hanns von Rohr)
    Grenadier-Regiment 725
    Grenadier-Regiment 735

---

1   Only those units involved in the Gothic Line campaign are listed in the Axis orders of battle that follow.

334.Infanterie-Division (Generalleutnant Hellmuth Böhlke)
  Grenadier-Regiment 754
  Grenadier-Regiment 755
  Grenadier-Regiment 756
305.Infanterie-Division (Generalleutnant Friedrich-Wilhelm Hauck)
  Grenadier-Regiment 576
  Grenadier-Regiment 577
  Grenadier-Regiment 578
44.Infanterie-Division 'Hoch und Deutschmeister' (Generalleutnant Hans-Günther von Rost)
  Grenadier-Regiment 131
  Grenadier-Regiment 132
  Reichsgrenadier-Regiment 'H.u.D.' (Grenadier-Regiment 134)
114.Jäger-Division (Generalmajor Hans-Joachim Ehlert)
  Jäger-Regiment 721
  Jäger-Regiment 741
LXXVI.Panzer-Korps (General der Panzertruppe Traugott Herr)
5.Gebirgs-Division (transferring to the Alpine front, not involved in the Gothic Line battles)
71.Infanterie-Division (Generalmajor Wilhelm Raapke)
  Grenadier-Regiment 191
  Grenadier-Regiment 194
  Grenadier-Regiment 211
1.Fallschirmjäger-Division (Generalleutnant Richard Heidrich)
  Fallschirmjäger-Regiment 1
  Fallschirmjäger-Regiment 3
  Fallschirmjäger-Regiment 4
278.Infanterie-Division (in the process of replacing 5.Gebirgs-Division) (Generalleutnant Harry Hoppe)
  Grenadier-Regiment 992
  Grenadier-Regiment 993
  Grenadier-Regiment 994
Korps Witthöft (General der Infanterie Joachim Witthöft)[2]
162.Infanterie-Division (Turkestanische) (Generalleutnant Ralph von Heygendorff)
  Infanterie-Regiment 303
  Infanterie-Regiment 314
  Infanterie-Regiment 329
98.Infanterie-Division (Generalmajor Alfred Reinhardt)
  Grenadier-Regiment 117
  Grenadier-Regiment 289
  Grenadier-Regiment 290

2   The Generalkommando Korps Witthöft was given several designations until officially named Befehlshaber Venetianische Küste (Venetian Coast Command) on 15 May.

AOK 14

(General der Panzertruppe Joachim Lemelsen, from 23 October 1944 Generalleutnant Heinz Ziegler)
Army reserves
90.Panzergrenadier-Division (Generalleutnant Ernst-Günther Baade)
  Panzergrenadier-Regiment 200
  Panzergrenadier-Regiment 361
362.Infanterie-Division (Generalleutnant Heinrich Greiner)
  Grenadier-Regiment 956
  Grenadier-Regiment 1059
  Grenadier-Regiment 1060
LXXV.Armee-Korps (General der Gebirgstruppe Hans Schlemmer)
Festungs-Brigade 135
20.Luftwaffe-Feld-Division (Generalmajor Wilhelm Crisolli, from 1 September 1944 Generalmajor Erich Fronhoefer)
  Jäger-Regiment 39
  Jäger-Regiment 40
16.SS-Panzergrenadier-Division 'Reichsführer-SS' (SS-Gruppenführer Max Simon, from 24 October 1944 SS-Oberführer Otto Baum)
  SS-Panzergrenadier-Regiment 35
  SS-Panzergrenadier-Regiment 36
XIV.Panzer-Korps (General der Panzertruppe Fridolin von Senger und Etterlin)
65.Infanterie-Division (Generalleutnant Hellmuth Pfeiffer)
  Grenadier-Regiment 145
  Grenadier-Regiment 146
  Grenadier-Regiment 147
26.Panzer-Division (Generalleutnant Eduard Crasemann)
  Panzer-Regiment 26
  Panzergrenadier-Regiment 9
  Panzergrenadier-Regiment 67
  Grenadier-Lehr-Brigade
I.Fallschirm-Korps (General der Flieger Alfred Schlemm)
29.Panzergrenadier-Division (Generalleutnant Fritz Polack)
  Panzergrenadier-Regiment 15
  Panzergrenadier-Regiment 71
4.Fallschirmjäger-Division (Generalmajor Heinrich Trettner)
  Fallschirmjäger-Regiment 10
  Fallschirmjäger-Regiment 11
  Fallschirmjäger-Regiment 12
356.Infanterie-Division (Generalleutnant Karl Fauelenbach)
  Grenadier-Regiment 869
  Grenadier-Regiment 870
  Grenadier-Regiment 871

ORDERS OF BATTLE, 1 NOVEMBER 1944

ALLIED

Supreme Allied Commander, Mediterranean Theatre (General Sir Henry Maitland Wilson, from 12 December 1944 Field Marshal Sir Harold Alexander)
Allied Armies in Italy – renamed 15th Army Group on 16 December 1944 (from 16 December 1944 Lieutenant-General Mark W. Clark, promoted to general on 10 March 1945)

BR EIGHTH ARMY

(Lieutenant-General Sir Richard McCreery)
Porter Force
Army reserves
NZ 2nd Infantry Division (Lieutenant-General Sir Bernard Freyberg VC)
  NZ 4th Armoured Brigade
  NZ 5th Infantry Brigade
  NZ 6th Infantry Brigade

BR 56th Infantry Division (Major-General John Y. Whitfield)
  BR 167th Infantry Brigade
  BR 169th Infantry Brigade
  BR 24th Guards Brigade (from February 1945)
CDN I Corps (Lieutenant-General Eedson L.M. Burns, from 10 November 1944 Lieutenant-General Charles Foulkes)
CDN 5th Armoured Division (Major-General Bertram C. Hoffmeister)
  CDN 5th Armoured Brigade
  CDN 11th Infantry Brigade
  CDN 12th Infantry Brigade
CDN 1st Infantry Division (Major-General Christopher Vokes, from 1 December 1944 Major-General Harry Foster)
  CDN 1st Infantry Brigade
  CDN 2nd Infantry Brigade
  CDN 3rd Infantry Brigade
CDN 1st Armoured Brigade
BR 21st Tank Brigade

BR X Corps HQ (Lieutenant-General Sir Richard McCreery, from 6 November 1944 Major-General John L.I. Hawkesworth)[3]
POL II Corps (Lieutenant-General Władysław Anders)
POL 3rd Carpathian Infantry Division (Major-General Bronisław Duch)
    POL 1st Carpathian Rifle Brigade
    POL 2nd Carpathian Rifle Brigade
POL 5th Kresowa Infantry Division (Major-General Nikodem Sulik-Sarnowski)
    POL 5th Wilenska Infantry Brigade
    POL 6th Lwowska Infantry Brigade
POL 2nd Armoured Brigade
BR V Corps (Lieutenant-General Charles F. Keightley)
BR 4th Infantry Division (Major-General Alfred D. Ward)[4]
    BR 10th Infantry Brigade
    BR 12th Infantry Brigade
    BR 28th Infantry Brigade
BR 46th Infantry Division (Major-General John L.I. Hawkesworth, from 6 November 1944 Major-General C.E. Weir)
    BR 128th Infantry Brigade
    BR 138th Infantry Brigade
    BR 139th Infantry Brigade
    BR 2nd Armoured Brigade
IND 10th Infantry Division (Major-General Denys W. Reid)
    IND 10th Infantry Brigade
    IND 20th Infantry Brigade
    IND 25th Infantry Brigade
    IND 43rd Gurkha Lorried Infantry Brigade
BR 25th Tank Brigade

US FIFTH ARMY

(Lieutenant-General Mark W. Clark, from 16 December 1944 Lieutenant-General Lucian K. Truscott)
US Task Force 92 (from 8 November 1944):
US 92nd Infantry Division (Major-General Edward M. Almond)
    US 365th Infantry Regiment
    US 370th Infantry Regiment
    US 371st Infantry Regiment
    US 366th Infantry Regiment (attached from 19 November 1944 to 25 February 1945)
US II Corps (Major-General Geoffrey T. Keyes)
US 1st Armored Division (Major-General Vernon E. Pritchard)
    US Combat Command A
    US Combat Command B
US 34th Infantry Division (Major-General Charles L. Bolté)
    US 133rd Infantry Regiment
    US 135th Infantry Regiment
    US 168th Infantry Regiment
US 85th Infantry Division (Major-General John B. Coulter)
    US 337th Infantry Regiment
    US 338th Infantry Regiment
    US 339th Infantry Regiment
US 88th Infantry Division (Major-General Paul W. Kendall)
    US 349th Infantry Regiment
    US 350th Infantry Regiment
    US 351st Infantry Regiment
US 91st Infantry Division (Major-General William G. Livesay)
    US 361st Infantry Regiment
    US 362nd Infantry Regiment
    US 363rd Infantry Regiment
US IV Corps (Lieutenant-General Willis D. Crittenberger)
1st Infantry Division, Brazilian Expeditionary Force (Força Expedicionária Brasileira) (Major-General João Batista Mascarenhas de Moraes)
    1st Infantry Regiment
    6th Infantry Regiment
    11th Infantry Regiment

SA 6th Armoured Division (Major-General William H.E. Poole)
    SA 11th Armoured Brigade
    SA 12th Motorized Infantry Brigade
    SA 13th Motorized Infantry Brigade (from 13 January 1945)
    BR 24th Guards Brigade (detached February 1945)
US Task Force 45 (Brigadier-General Cecil L. Rutledge)
US 10th Mountain Division (Major-General George P. Hays) (from 24 January 1945)
    US 85th Mountain Infantry Regiment
    US 86th Mountain Infantry Regiment
    US 87th Mountain Infantry Regiment
BR XIII Corps (Lieutenant-General Sidney C. Kirkman)
BR 6th Armoured Division (Major-General Horatius Murray)
    BR 26th Armoured Brigade
    BR 1st Guards Brigade
    BR 61st Infantry Brigade
BR 1st Infantry Division (Major-General Charles F. Loewen)
    BR 2nd Infantry Brigade
    BR 3rd Infantry Brigade
    BR 66th Infantry Brigade
BR 78th Infantry Division (Major-General R.K. Arbuthnott) (from 5 October 1944)
    BR 11th Infantry Brigade
    BR 36th Infantry Brigade
    BR 38th Infantry Brigade
IND 8th Infantry Division (Major-General Dudley Russell)
    IND 17th Infantry Brigade
    IND 19th Infantry Brigade
    IND 21st Infantry Brigade

AXIS

Heeresgruppe Süd (Generaloberst Heinrich von Vietinghoff, from 15 January 1945 Generalfeldmarschall Albert Kesselring)

AOK 10

(General der Panzertruppe Joachim Lemelsen, from 15 February 1945 General der Panzertruppe Traugott Herr)
Army reserve
90.Panzergrenadier-Division (Generalleutnant Ernst-Günther Baade, from 26 December 1944 Generalmajor Heinrich Baron von Behr)
    Panzergrenadier-Regiment 200
    Panzergrenadier-Regiment 361
I.Fallschirm-Korps (General der Flieger Alfred Schlemm, from 18 November 1944 Generalleutnant Richard Heidrich, from 23 January 1945 Generalleutnant Hellmuth Böhlke)
94.Infanterie-Division (Generalleutnant Bernhard Steinmetz)
    Grenadier-Regiment 267
    Grenadier-Regiment 274
    Grenadier-Regiment 276
16.SS-Panzergrenadier-Division 'Reichsführer-SS' (SS-Oberführer Otto Baum)
    SS-Panzergrenadier-Regiment 35
    SS-Panzergrenadier-Regiment 36
4.Fallschirmjäger-Division (Generalmajor Heinrich Trettner)
    Fallschirmjäger-Regiment 10
    Fallschirmjäger-Regiment 11
    Fallschirmjäger-Regiment 12
XIV.Panzer-Korps (General der Panzertruppe Fridolin von Senger und Etterlin)
65.Infanterie-Division (Generalleutnant Hellmuth Pfeiffer)
    Grenadier-Regiment 145
    Grenadier-Regiment 146
    Grenadier-Regiment 147
29.Panzergrenadier-Division (Generalleutnant Fritz Polack)
    Panzergrenadier-Regiment 15
    Panzergrenadier-Regiment 71

---

3   HQ subsequently moved to Greece.
4   To Greece December 1944.

362.Infanterie-Division (Generalleutnant Heinrich Greiner)
  Grenadier-Regiment 956
  Grenadier-Regiment 1059
  Grenadier-Regiment 1060
1.Fallschirmjäger-Division (Generalleutnant Richard Heidrich, from
  18 November 1944 Generalmajor Karl-Lothar Schulz)
  Fallschirmjäger-Regiment 1
  Fallschirmjäger-Regiment 3
  Fallschirmjäger-Regiment 4
98.Infanterie-Division (Generalleutnant Alfred Reinhardt)
  Grenadier-Regiment 117 (rebuilt from Grenadier Lehr Brigade)
  Grenadier-Regiment 289
  Grenadier-Regiment 290
334.Infanterie-Division (Generalleutnant Hellmuth Böhlke)
  Grenadier-Regiment 754
  Grenadier-Regiment 755
  Grenadier-Regiment 756
42.Jäger-Division (Generalleutnant Walter Jost)
  Jäger-Regiment 25
  Jäger-Regiment 40

**LXXVI.Panzer-Korps (General der Panzertruppe
Traugott Herr, from 26 December 1944 General der
Panzertruppe Gerhard Graf von Schwerin)**
715.Infanterie-Division (Generalmajor Hanns von Rohr)
  Grenadier-Regiment 725
  Grenadier-Regiment 735
305.Infanterie-Division (Generalmajor Friedrich-Wilhelm Hauck, in
  December 1944 command temporarily held by Oberst Friedrich
  Trompeter, from 29 December 1944 Generalmajor Friedrich von
  Schellwitz)
  Grenadier-Regiment 576
  Grenadier-Regiment 577
  Grenadier-Regiment 578
356.Infanterie-Division (Generalleutnant Karl Fauelenbach, from
  12 December 1944 Generalmajor Claus Kühl)
  Grenadier-Regiment 869
  Grenadier-Regiment 870
  Grenadier-Regiment 871
278.Infanterie-Division (Generalleutnant Harry Hoppe)
  Grenadier-Regiment 992

  Grenadier-Regiment 993
  Grenadier-Regiment 994
26.Panzer-Division (Generalleutnant Eduard Crasemann)
  Panzer-Regiment 26
  Panzergrenadier-Regiment 9
  Panzergrenadier-Regiment 67
20.Luftwaffe-Feld-Division (Generalmajor Erich Fronhoefer)
  Jäger-Regiment 39
  Jäger-Regiment 40

**Korps Witthöft – renamed 26 November 1944 LXXIII.Armee-
Korps (General der Infanterie Joachim Witthöft)**
114.Jäger-Division (Generalmajor Hans-Joachim Ehlert)
  Jäger-Regiment 721
  Jäger-Regiment 741
162.Infanterie-Division (Turkestanische) (Generalleutnant Ralph von
  Heygendorff)
  Infanterie-Regiment 303
  Infanterie-Regiment 314
  Infanterie-Regiment 329

AOK 14

(General der Artillerie Heinz Ziegler, from 22 November 1944
  General der Panzertruppe Traugott Herr, from 12 December
  1944 Generalleutnant Kurt von Tippelskirch, from 23 February
  1945 General der Panzertruppe Joachim Lemelsen)
**Armee-Korps-Lombardia (deployed on the Ligurian Coast)
LI.Gebirgs-Armee-Korps (General der Gebirgstruppe Valentin
Feuerstein)**
IT 4th Mountain Division 'Monte Rosa' (Major-General Mario Carloni)
  IT 1st Alpini Regiment
  IT 2nd Alpini Regiment
232.Bodenständige-Infanterie-Division (from December 1944
  Generalleutnant Eccard Freiherr von Gablenz)
  Grenadier-Regiment 1043
  Grenadier-Regiment 1044
  Grenadier-Regiment 1045
148.Infanterie-Division (Generalleutnant Otto Fretter-Pico)
  Grenadier-Regiment 281
  Grenadier-Regiment 285
  Grenadier-Regiment 286

Strategic situation, 25 August 1944, and Allied plans

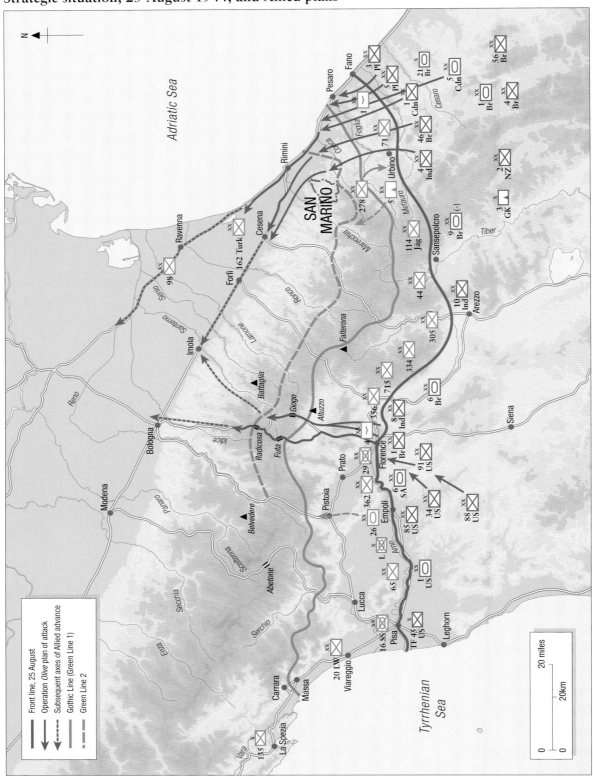

N

Adriatic Sea

Fano

Pesaro

3 Pl

1 Cdn

5 Pl

21 Br

56 Br

Cdn 5

1 Br

4 Br

Rimini

Foglia

1

71

46 Br

2 NZ

Urbino

4 Ind

Cesena

278

Metauro

5

3 GK

Tiber

Ravenna

Forlì

162 Turk

Marecchia

Conca

SAN MARINO

114 Jäg

Sansepolcro

9 Br

98

Senio

Santerno

Imola

Ronco

Lamone

Falterona

44

305

10 Ind

Arezzo

334

715

Siena

Reno

Santerno

Bologna

Idice

Radicosa

Futa

Il Giogo

Altuzzo

Battaglia

336

1 Br

8 Ind

6 Br

Florence

91 US

Panaro

Modena

Belvedere

Prato

Pistoia

29

362

6 SA

34 US

88 US

Secchia

Scoltenna

Abetone

26

Empoli

Arno

85 US

Enza

Serchio

Lucca

65

L

1 US

La Spezia

135

Carrara

Massa

20 LW

Viareggio

16 SS

Pisa

TF 45

45 US

Leghorn

Tyrrhenian Sea

20 miles

20km

Legend

Front line, 25 August

Operation *Olive* plan of attack

Subsequent axes of Allied advance

Gothic Line (Green Line 1)

Green Line 2

26

OPPOSING PLANS

ALLIED

By February 1944, BR Eighth Army's staff had already evaluated the possibilities of a breakthrough into the Po valley, reaching the conclusion that there were two alternatives: an attack across the mountains along the Florence–Bologna axis, or an attack on the eastern coast. The Florence–Bologna axis was deemed best suited to a swift advance aimed at preventing prolonged German resistance, to be achieved using feints and deception measures, which would suggest an advance on the eastern coast and a landing in north-west Italy.

In July, as the Allied armies advanced towards Florence, Field Marshal Alexander gave his support to the idea of the offensive, developed by General Leese and eventually accepted by General Clark. The idea was to attack north-west of Florence towards Bologna, widen the front and then advance to Ferrara to establish a bridgehead on the Po. At the end of July, as the Germans withdrew to the Arno River and units were withdrawn for the *Dragoon* landings, the plan was fleshed out. On 28 July, Leese issued the relevant orders, the regrouping starting two days later. The plan to reach Bologna called for two British corps to attack from the Florence area, with US Fifth Army attacking along a parallel axis on the west coast.

Rimini seen from the air in September 1944 during an Allied bombing raid; a B-25 bomber is visible at upper left. The terrain to the right (north) was deemed better suited to armoured warfare. (NARA)

US General Mark Clark with his assistant, Technician Fourth Grade Geraldine Horne, on 1 September 1944. (PhotoQuest/Getty Images)

However, on 4 August, Leese met Alexander to suggest a completely new plan: BR Eighth Army was to attack on the eastern coast, and US Fifth Army would attack in support along the Florence–Bologna axis. This sudden change presented many issues. Apart from having to regroup forces again, which would take time and create confusion, it precisely matched the deception plan. No satisfactory explanation has been given for the change of plans, which some have put down to BR Eighth Army's ('tank heavy') unwillingness to fight in the mountains. In addition, Leese's jealousy towards Clark suggested the latter would take all the glory for the breakthrough into the Po valley, should the two armies fight shoulder to shoulder.

In fact, BR Eighth Army's staff had already outlined the pros and cons of this move. The eastern coastal terrain was better suited to armoured warfare, even if the enemy could create a series of defensive lines in the area. Also, the Germans could switch its reserves from one area to another, meaning that if BR Eighth Army was caught by winter in the Ravenna–Forlì area, the attack would bog down. On the other hand, it was now clear that the deception had not worked and that the Germans expected the main enemy thrust to come along the Florence–Bologna axis. According to estimates, this enabled BR Eighth Army, with nine divisions or equivalent and 600–750 tanks, to face an opponent with only seven divisions (some of which were weak) and 230 tanks.

Clark asked for, and received, BR XIII Corps' attachment to US Fifth Army to secure the right flank, and the final plan was outlined. The BR Eighth Army was to attack with CDN I Corps to break through the Gothic Line defences, the weak Polish Corps supporting its right wing. The BR V Corps would be the pursuit corps, advancing to the left of CDN I Corps towards Bologna as the latter advanced towards Rimini and Ravenna. In the meantime, US Fifth Army was to attack on the Florence–Bologna axis to prevent the Germans from redeploying their forces and to break through the Gothic Line as well.

On 6 August, the orders for Operation *Olive* were issued; regrouping delayed its start (along with Operation *Dragoon*) for about ten days, from mid-August to the 25th.

AXIS

On 4 June 1944, as the Allies entered Rome, Kesselring informed Hitler that he wanted to fight a delaying withdrawal in central Italy to buy time and construct the Gothic Line. Hitler did not agree with this plan, and five days later made his mind clear: the Gothic Line was not ready, and a protracted defence further south in central Italy was therefore necessary. On 14 June, Hitler stated that the Gothic Line would form the last stand before the Po River valley, which lies in northern Italy, and losing it would mean losing the entire country. This meant holding central Italy for as long as possible and, to make things clearer, the next day he ordered a change to the name of the Gothic Line to the Green Line.

The Allied advance left no margin for discussion, as the development of the situation imposed a withdrawal, sooner or later, to the Green Line. Eventually, on 5 July, the OKH (Oberkommando der Wehrmacht – High Command of the Armed Forces) authorized Kesselring to defend the Green Line as the last main defensive line in Italy, while holding on for as long as possible in central Italy. Three days later, Kesselring reassured the OKH that this was his intention, making clear at the same time his concern over possible landings on either the eastern or the western coasts that could jeopardize the withdrawal.

Exhausted German POWs held at Castel del Rio, Emilia-Romagna, in late October 1944. One of the Allied aims of the Gothic Line campaign was to divert German troops from other fronts. (Mondadori via Getty Images)

That the Gothic/Green Line was considered the last stand in Italy is confirmed by the fact that on 27 July, Hitler ordered the start of the construction of the Voralpen Stellung (Pre-Alps Position), a new defensive line south of the northern Alps. Two days later, Heeresgruppe C headquarters issued orders for Operation *Herbstnebel* (*Autumn Fog*), the withdrawal to the northern Alps and the abandonment of Italy.

The Allied landings in southern France and the Allied entry into Florence, followed by the withdrawal of two Panzergrenadier divisions to the Western Front, compelled Kesselring, on 22 August, to accelerate the withdrawal to the Green Line. At this point, knowing that no reinforcements were forthcoming for the Italian front (other than the four Italian divisions training in Germany), he faced a complicated situation. The landings in southern France opened a new front in the Western Alps, while an Allied landing in Italy could not be ruled out. This required the use of troops to garrison all these potential fronts, while defending the main front. Since German intelligence had failed to spot the last-minute BR Eighth Army redeployment, there was no certainty as to whence the enemy attack would come, and the Germans believed this would take place on a wide front with a focus on the Adriatic coast.

US soldiers inspecting a destroyed Marder III from 71.Infanterie-Division. The terrain made up for the limited availability of German tanks and anti-tank guns. (Photo 12/Alamy)

The only possible strategy was defence in depth. Not only did Kesselring order the building of the Green Line II while holding an advanced line on the Metauro River on 5 July, but construction of an intermediate line facing BR Eighth Army was also begun. The idea was to buy time while waiting for the arrival of autumn, which would slow the Allied advance, preventing a collapse that would make Operation *Herbstnebel* unavoidable.

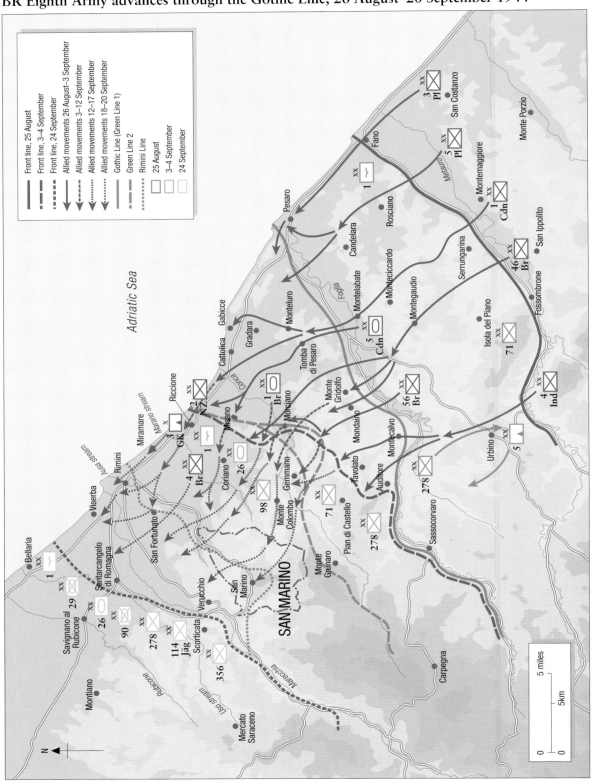

Front line, 25 August
Front line, 3–4 September
Front line, 24 September
Allied movements 26 August–3 September
Allied movements 3–12 September
Allied movements 12–17 September
Allied movements 18–20 September
Gothic Line (Green Line 1)
Green Line 2
Rimini Line
25 August
3–4 September
24 September

Adriatic Sea

San Costanzo
Monte Porzio
Fano
San Ippolito
Montemaggiore
Serrungarina
Fossombrone
Pesaro
Candelara
Rosciano
Montelabate
Monteciccardo
Montegaudio
Isola del Piano
Gabicce
Monteluro
Gradara
Cattolica
Tomba di Pesaro
Monte Gridolfo
Riccione
Morciano
Mondaino
Urbino
Misano
Montecalvo
Rimini
Coriano
Gemmano
Tavolato
Auditore
Viserba
San Fortunato
Monte Colombo
Pian di Castello
Sassocorvaro
Bellaria
Verucchio
Mercato
Monte Grunaro
Savignano al Rubicone
SAN MARINO
Santarcangelo di Romagna
San Marino
Scorticata
Carpegna
Montiano
Mercato Saraceno

Marano stream
Alsa stream
Miramare
Conca
Foglia
Metauro
Uso stream
Rubicone
Marecchia

N

5 miles
5km

30

THE CAMPAIGN

BR EIGHTH ARMY BREACHES THE GOTHIC LINE

At 2300hrs on 24 August 1944, CDN I Corps moved through the Polish Corps' positions to approach the Metauro River, which was soon crossed to establish bridgeheads. Until 27 August CDN 1st Division faced occasional resistance from elements of the withdrawing 71.Infanterie-Division, with the terrain proving equally problematic: roads filled with craters, buildings demolished to block the route, gullies and knolls marking a broken terrain made up of isolated hills. The first serious resistance was met on 27–28 August as the Canadians encountered elements of 1.Fallschirmjäger-Division and the 71.Infanterie-Division defending Monteciccardo.

The POL 5th Kresowa Division was held up on the Adriatic coast while, to the left, BR V Corps' 46th Division managed to keep up with the Canadian pace of advance, although IND 4th Division's advance was delayed until 29 August.

On 28–29 August, the Polish and Canadian troops faced a last German defensive line along the Arzilla stream, south of the Foglia River, with elements from 71.Infanterie-Division and Fallschirmjäger-Regiment 4 defending the twin hill towns of Monteciccardo and Montegaudio. The German positions were attacked after heavy bombardment of the area, and as their defences were overrun, withdrawal became necessary. Between 28 and 29 August, the Canadian and Polish troops, as well as the British, were now in sight of the Gothic Line (as the Allies still called it) defences along the Foglia. This turned out to be a major tactical advantage.

Not only had air reconnaissance already identified three-quarters of the Gothic Line positions, mostly running along the main road north of the Foglia,

An M7 Priest 105mm SP gun on a road near Mondaino, 6 September 1944. This is the kind of road BR Eighth Army troops had to negotiate in order to redeploy on the Adriatic side of the Appenines. (Photo by Sgt Dawson/ Imperial War Museums via Getty Images)

CDN 1ST INFANTRY DIVISION TAKES MONTE DELLA MATTERA, 26 AUGUST 1944 (PP. 32–33)

After crossing the Metauro River, the Canadians had to seize a series of hills in order to pave the way for their advance to the Foglia River and the Gothic Line. In the morning of 26 August, CDN 2nd Brigade's Seaforth Highlanders of Canada Regiment easily crossed the river, sweeping away the rearguards of the German 71.Infanterie-Division south of Monte della Mattera. C Company started approaching the southern slopes of Monte della Mattera, deploying its 13th Platoon to assault the narrow incline.

As it deployed and started to advance at 1140hrs, German machine-gun fire started coming from the top from well-placed nests (**1**). Soon a Sturmgeschütz SP gun (**2**) joined in, firing on the men of 13th Platoon. The Canadians had no other choice than to crawl their way up the slope, protected by the fire of a Bren Gun team (**3**). A Churchill Mk IV (**4**) from C Squadron of BR 145th Regiment, RAC, part of BR 21st Tank Brigade supporting CDN 1st Infantry Division, began firing on the German positions and at the Sturmgeschütz, which soon withdrew. The advance was very slow, and it took 50 minutes for the men of 13th Platoon to reach the summit of Monte della Mattera, inching their way forward as they tried to avoid the enemy fire. Once on the summit, they found that the bulk of the German defenders had gone, leaving them to take only 15 wounded prisoners, for three of their own wounded. The soldier on the right of this illustration, armed with a Thompson SMG (**5**), displays the Seaforth Highlanders of Canada Regiment title on his shoulder, and the red rectangle denoting the CDN 2nd Brigade (**6**).

but Allied troops could also take advantage of the excellent observation area provided by the high ground to the south. Even though the Gothic Line appeared stronger than expected with its anti-tank ditches covered by machine-gun nests surrounded by barbed wire, it was soon clear that only the 'Panther' turrets gave depth to it. Twenty-four of these were spotted, noticeably all without supporting infantry positions. To soften the enemy defences on the 29th, 1,600 tons of bombs were dropped, with air units providing close support until the following day. In the meantime, BR Eighth Army's artillery was reinforced with NZ 2nd Division supporting CDN I Corps, and BR 56th and 1st Armoured divisions supporting BR V Corps. Fire plans were laid down, helped by observation and by the disposition of defences.

The speed of BR Eighth Army's initial advance led to a planned breakthrough of the Gothic Line on 26 August. Units were moved forward, POL 3rd Carpathian Division advancing across the 5th Kresowa, CDN 5th Armoured moving to the left of BR 1st Infantry and BR 56th Infantry Division and BR 7th Armoured Brigade being inserted between IND 4th and BR 46th divisions. The NZ 2nd Division and GK 3rd Mountain Brigade were ordered to assemble and be ready from 30 August, while BR 4th Division was left in reserve.

Convinced that the Germans had either been taken by surprise or that they were planning to withdraw from Italy, on 29 August General Leese decided that the three corps under his command should not rest, but rather attempt to crash through the Gothic Line defences. Patrols were sent forward to the Foglia, followed by the infantry companies. That night, General Burns ordered the Canadian divisions to break through along the Tavullia–Monteluro axis, with the attack commencing on the afternoon of 30 August.

The Germans had indeed been caught completely by surprise. By mid-August, in the wake of the Allied landings in southern France, Kesselring had been focusing his attention on the Western Alps where he had committed the 90.Panzergrenadier-Division, while at the same time relieving the 3. and 15.Panzergrenadier divisions (replaced by 65.Infanterie-Division and 305.Infanterie-Division), which were bound for the Western Front. Only on 23 August did the 278.Infanterie-Division begin to replace the 5.Gebirgs-Division, which was intended to replace the 90.Panzergrenadier-Division in the Alps, while the 1.Fallschirmjäger-Division deployed along the front close to the 278.Infanterie-Division. This left the 98.Infanterie-Division as AOK 10's only reserve, the 26.Panzer-Division being subordinated only on the 27th, its commitment subject to Kesselring's approval.

Having failed to detect BR Eighth Army's redeployment to the Adriatic coast, AOK 10's HQ did not appraise the situation correctly, believing that the enemy advance was merely an attempt to keep up with the German withdrawal. The idea was to defend the forward and intermediate positions before withdrawing to Green I, and only on 26–27 August did the heavy bombing of the Green I positions reveal the veracity of BR Eighth Army's intent, even though Kesselring remained sceptical.

Still, facing repeated requests from AOK 10's chief of staff for reinforcements, Kesselring recommended recalling General von Vietinghoff from leave and at the same time agreeing to speed up the replacement of 29.Panzergrenadier-Division with 334.Infanterie-Division, while putting 98.Infanterie-Division under direct command of LXXVI.Panzer-Korps.

THE CANADIANS BREACH THE GOTHIC LINE, 30 AUGUST–3 SEPTEMBER 1944

After crossing the Foglia River, on the afternoon of 30 August the CDN 5th Armoured and CDN 1st Infantry divisions attacked the Gothic Line positions south-west of Pesaro. After a difficult start, the Canadians managed to break through the German defences and, thanks to their relentless advance and skilled infantry–tank cooperation, overcame the reinforcements from 26.Panzer-Division.
On 2 September, the Germans withdrew east, leaving the road to the Adriatic, and to the Conca River south-east of Rimini, open to the Canadians.

SAN GI
IN MAR

PIETRAFITTA

MONTE
MARRONE

TAVULLIA

IL BORGO

MONTECCHIO

POZZO
ALTO

OSTERIA
NUOVA

MONTELABBATE

BORGO
SANTA MARIA

ANTI-TA
DITCH

FOGLIA
RIVER

I CDN ✕✕✕

BURNS

ALLIED

1. Princess Patricia Canadian Light Infantry (PPCLI), 2nd Brigade, CDN 1st Infantry Division
2. Seaforth of Canada, 2nd Brigade, CDN 1st Infantry Division
3. Loyal Edmonton, 2nd Brigade, CDN 1st Infantry Division
4. West Nova Scotia, 3rd Brigade, CDN 1st Infantry Division
5. Royal 22nd Regiment, 3rd Brigade, CDN 1st Infantry Division
6. 1st Armoured Car Regiment (Dragoons), divisional recce, CDN 1st Infantry Division
7. 9th Armoured Regiment (British Columbia Dragoons), 5th Armoured Brigade, CDN 5th Armoured Division
8. 5th Armoured Regiment (8th Princess Louise's (New Brunswick) Hussars), 5th Armoured Brigade, CDN 5th Armoured Division
9. Cape Breton Highlanders, 11th Brigade, CDN 5th Armoured Division
10. Irish Regiment of Canada, 11th Brigade, CDN 5th Armoured Division

11. Perth Regiment, 11th Brigade, CDN 5th Armoured Division
12. 4th Princess Louise Dragoon Guards, CDN 5th Armoured Division (assigned to 11th Brigade on 25 August 1944)
13. Westminster Regiment, 12th Brigade, CDN 5th Armoured Division
14. 1st Light Anti-Aircraft Battalion (Lanark & Renfrew Scottish Regiment), 12th Brigade, CDN 5th Armoured Division
15. 3rd Armoured Car Regiment (Horse Guards), divisional recce, CDN 5th Armoured Division
16. 145th Regiment RAC, BR 21st Tank Brigade
17. 12th Royal Tank Regiment, BR 21st Tank Brigade
18. 48th Royal Tank Regiment, BR 21st Tank Brigade
19. 2nd Armoured Regiment (Lord Strathcona's Horse), 5th Armoured Brigade, CDN 5th Armoured Division
20. Royal Canadian Regiment, 1st Brigade, CDN 1st Infantry Division

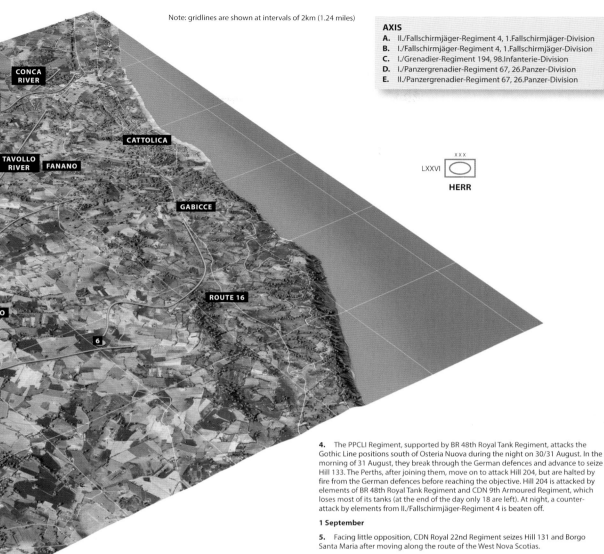

Note: gridlines are shown at intervals of 2km (1.24 miles)

LXXVI

HERR

CONCA RIVER

CATTOLICA

TAVOLLO RIVER FANANO

GABICCE

ROUTE 16

6

4. The PPCLI Regiment, supported by BR 48th Royal Tank Regiment, attacks the Gothic Line positions south of Osteria Nuova during the night on 30/31 August. In the morning of 31 August, they break through the German defences and advance to seize Hill 133. The Perths, after joining them, move on to attack Hill 204, but are halted by fire from the German defences before reaching the objective. Hill 204 is attacked by elements of BR 48th Royal Tank Regiment and CDN 9th Armoured Regiment, which loses most of its tanks (at the end of the day only 18 are left). At night, a counter-attack by elements from II./Fallschirmjäger-Regiment 4 is beaten off.

1 September

5. Facing little opposition, CDN Royal 22nd Regiment seizes Hill 131 and Borgo Santa Maria after moving along the route of the West Nova Scotias.

6. After two unsuccessful attacks, carried out during the night by the PPCLI, in the morning of 1 September the Seaforths succeed in taking Pozzo Alto. They continue their advance to reach the foot of Hill 119.

7. The CDN 4th Princess Louise Dragoons, supported by CDN 2nd Armoured Regiment, move from the area of Hill 204 (Pozzo Alto) towards the crossroads east of Tavullia. They catch elements from I./Panzergrenadier-Regiment 67 regrouping to counter-attack, wiping out many of them en route to reaching their objective.

8. The CDN Loyal Edmonton Regiment, supported by BR 12th Royal Tank Regiment and under the cover of Canadian and New Zealand artillery, advances from Pozzo Alto to Monteluro, which is taken after they discover that the Germans have withdrawn.

9. The PPCLI, followed by BR 48th Royal Tank Regiment and BR 12th Royal Tank Regiment, advance at speed to the north with the aim of cutting the railway in two to the south-east of Gradara. Meanwhile, the Loyal Edmonton, supported by elements from BR 12th Royal Tank Regiment, advances to the west towards Monteluro and Fanano, west of Gradara. Thanks to the German withdrawal, the only opposition encountered comprises fire coming from Gradara Castle. The advance succeeds and enables A Squadron of CDN 1st Armoured Car Regiment to reach Route 16 south of Gabicce.

2–3 September

10. The CDN 1st Light AA Battalion and the Westminster Regiment, both supported by CDN 3rd Armoured Car Regiment, advance along parallel paths from the Tavullia area towards San Giovanni in Marignano. Their progress paves the way for the speedy advance of D Squadron, CDN 1st Armoured Car Regiment, which pushes on along the road, and in the early hours of 3 September establishes a bridgehead on the Conca River, which is then consolidated by the Royal Canadian Regiment.

▼ EVENTS

30 August

1. At 1730hrs, the Cape Breton Highlanders, supported by the 5th Armoured Regiment and the Perth Regiment, attack the German positions at Montecchio. The Cape Bretons are repulsed by the defences at Hill 120 and are forced to withdraw after losing 19 killed and 46 wounded. The Perths succeed in breaking through the German defences and seize Hill 111, which enables them to attack Hill 147 from the rear and capture it at the end of the day.

2. Halted by minefields and enemy fire, the West Nova Scotias are forced to withdraw before reaching their target after losing 20 killed and 56 wounded.

31 August

3. Thanks to the breakthrough achieved by the Perths, the Irish Regiment is able to move to the rear of Hill 120, which is then seized in the afternoon together with the support of the Cape Bretons attacking from the south. In the aftermath, the Cape Breton Highlanders advance northwards, reaching Monte Marrone with the support of CDN 5th Armoured Regiment.

Churchill tanks of BR 51st Royal Tank Regiment advance near Isola del Piano, Pesaro, in support of BR 138th Brigade's attack during the advance to the Gothic Line. (© Imperial War Museum, NA 18088)

On 28 August, the Germans captured Leese's order of the day for Operation *Olive*, just as Kesselring, dismayed by the sudden withdrawal of 1.Fallschirmjäger Division and 71.Infanterie-Division, realized what was actually happening. Directives were immediately issued to both AOKs 10 and 14; the former was able to release the 26.Panzer-Division, and the latter was ordered to speed up the release of 29.Panzergrenadier Division, while also transferring the 20.Luftwaffe-Feld-Division to the Adriatic along with Flak and artillery units. On the 29th, both the 1.Fallschirmjäger-Division and the 71.Infanterie-Division were authorized to withdraw to Green I, with the rest of AOK 10 withdrawing on the night of 30 August – bearing in mind this was to be Germany's 'last line of defence' in Italy.

Meanwhile, CDN 1st Division's attack on the afternoon of 30 August did not begin well, as one battalion got stuck in a minefield and was unable to cross the Foglia. Only during the night was the division able to cross the river and establish a bridgehead, beating off a counter-attack by Fallschirmjäger-Regiment 4. The CDN 5th Armoured Division, after establishing a bridgehead near Montecchio on the 30th, advanced inland towards Tavullia the following day. On 1 September, the division caught 26.Panzer-Division's Panzergrenadier-Regiment 67 in the open, which was regrouping to counter-attack. The ensuing Canadian attack smashed it, inflicting heavy losses, just as CDN 1st Division was advancing towards Monteluro.

To the right the Polish units were not yet ready to advance, while to the left of CDN I Corps, BR V Corps had also succeeded in establishing a bridgehead. Facing no continuous line of defence, just isolated positions, BR 46th Division crossed the river with two brigades facing the Montegridolfo complex, which blocked the way to Marciano and the Conca River. Meanwhile, IND 4th Division, after crossing the Foglia on the night of 29/30 August, easily seized Monte della Croce and held it against 71.Infanterie-Division's counter-attacks, thanks to the support of the tanks of BR 6th RTR. On 31 August, a concentric attack on Montecalvo led to the breaching of the Gothic Line, just as BR 46th Division did by seizing Montegridolfo and Mondaino.

On 31 August, BR Eighth Army focused on exploiting the breakthroughs; CDN I Corps was ordered to advance towards the coast and establish a bridgehead on the Conca by using mixed tank and infantry formations, such as CDN 2nd Infantry Brigade cooperating with BR 21st Tank Brigade. That night, after an intense bombardment, the Canadians attacked Monteluro, only to find that the Germans had vacated it, making it clear that the skilled collaboration between armour and infantry had achieved the breakthrough. This enabled a speedy advance towards the coast, with CDN 5th Armoured Division following the 1st Division on 2 September and its 1st Dragoons crossing the Conca that same night. At the same time, the Polish Corps advanced, pushing 1.Fallschirmjäger-Division to evacuate Pesaro, which was

An M10 tank destroyer and British infantry move along a dirt road near Pesaro in late August 1944. The photo clearly shows the kind of terrain and climate facing BR Eighth Army soldiers during the early stages of the campaign. (© Imperial War Museum, NA 18091)

then seized on the 2nd. By the next day, a bridgehead had been established on the Conca.

BR Eighth Army's successful right-flank advance was followed by that of BR V Corps, BR 46th Division of which, after clearing the Montegridolfo–Mondaino area, still faced resistance from 71.Infanterie-Division along with several counter-attacks, which led to heavy fighting. Only after the Canadian advance to the coast did Keightley order BR 1st Armoured Division to move forward and lead the corps' pursuit towards Coriano, and BR 46th Division to advance to the Montegridolfo–Marciano area, paving the way for BR 1st Armoured, before entering the corps reserve. At the same time, BR 56th Division was to advance toward Montecalvo–Monte Colombo and IND 4th Division was to advance toward Tavolato–Monte Grunaro.

On 2 September, BR 46th Division advanced east of Montegridolfo, by then facing little opposition, which enabled it to make contact with the Canadians 1.5km south of Marciano. Its vanguards reached the Conca River the next day, establishing a bridgehead, as the German defences at Montegridolfo collapsed. By 4 September, the road was open for the advance towards Coriano.

The BR 56th Division, after facing German opposition at Tavolato until its withdrawal on the night of 2 September, advanced with two brigades east of Gemmano, where it halted. With the withdrawal of 71.Infanterie-Division on the night of 3/4 September, which allowed IND 4th Division to seize Tavolato, the two divisions began to advance to the Gemmano–Pian di Castello ridges. However, BR 56th Division decided to avoid the Gemmano ridge and turned east instead, following the path of BR 46th Division across the Conca. On 4 September, as a new German defensive line was established

A 20mm Flakvierling gun in an anti-aircraft emplacement. Guns like this were mostly employed against Allied fighter-bombers, but could also be used against ground targets. (ullstein bild via Getty Images)

between Rimini and San Marino, both BR 46th and 56th divisions exploited the bridgehead at the same time that BR 1st Armoured Division moved forward after regrouping south of the Foglia.

At 1525hrs on 31 August, LXXVI.Panzer-Korps announced it had lost control of the Green I positions, leading Kesselring to report to the OKH that the Allies had unleashed a major offensive. There were several reasons for the sudden German collapse, including the absence of 1.Fallschirmjäger-Division's commander, General Heidrich, who was on leave, and 26.Panzer-Divisions's faulty counter-attack. The division, unfamiliar with the area, deployed piecemeal and suffered from a lack of initiative by its commander. A Panther tank battalion was rushed to LXXVI.Panzer-Korps along with the 98.Infanterie-Division, even though it was clear that 29.Panzergrenadier-Division could not redeploy before 4 September. This led to the impromptu solution of halting the redeployment of Gebirgsjäger-Regiment 100 (from 5.Gebirgsjäger-Division) to the Alps. The only available reserve was 20.Luftwaffe-Feld-Division.

After the Canadian breakthrough on 2 September, Kesselring authorized the withdrawal to the Green II line, too late for 1.Fallschirmjäger-Division, whose Fallschirmjäger-Regiment 1 was cut off at Gradara and had to fight its way back to rejoin the 26.Panzer-Division, losing one company and most of its heavy guns. Meanwhile, 98. and 71.Infanterie-Division established a defensive line on the axis Montegridolfo–Marciano–San Clemente to buy time and consolidate the Green II positions.

On 3 September, General Wentzell, chief of staff of AOK 10, toured the front to re-establish order. He deployed Gebirgsjäger-Regiment 100 at Gemmano and Panzergrenadier-Regiment 71 (29.Panzergrenadier-Division's only available unit) at Coriano, with its four tanks and four anti-tank guns. Kesselring and von Vietinghoff endorsed this decision, aimed at buying time to enable 90.Panzergrenadier-Division to arrive while 71.Infanterie-Division, which was supposed to be relieved by 356.Infanterie-Division, remained engaged at the front.

THE BATTLE FOR RIMINI

After establishing a bridgehead on the Conca, CDN 1st Division advanced along the Via Adriatica (the coastal route), but its progress was slowed by destroyed bridges. In the meantime, CDN 5th Armoured, advancing to the left, faced the German defences at Misano ridge. On 4 September, as generals Burns and Leese met, it was clear that the Germans were fighting a delaying action, which would require a direct Allied assault. It was decided that CDN 1st Division's 1st Infantry Brigade was to advance towards Riccione, while CDN 5th Armoured Division's 5th Armoured Brigade was to drive the Germans away from Misano. In fact, German resistance was stiffening, as a result of reinforcements and the eventual return from leave of General Heidrich. His 1.Fallschirmjäger-Division was reinforced by Grenadier-Regiment 117 and a *Kampfgruppe* from 162.Infanterie-Division, while 98.Infanterie-Division deployed in the line alongside (without replacing) the 71.Infanterie-Division, and 29.Panzergrenadier-Division's Panzergrenadier-Regiment 71 deployed at Coriano.

It was soon clear that the Germans were determined to hold their positions for as long as possible. The CDN 1st Division was halted at the outskirts of Riccione by a German strongpoint, and CDN 5th Armoured Division's advance to Misano was held up by the fire from the Coriano ridge, the control of which was key. With CDN 1st Division having lost some 300 men in the stretch between the Conca and Riccione, by 6 September it was clear that a major reorganization was needed. Thus, the Canadian attacks were halted.

Exploiting the advance of BR 46th Division, BR 1st Armoured Division's 2nd Armoured Brigade eventually crossed the Conca at 0130hrs on 4 September, making contact with BR 4th Division later that same morning. The excitement of an easy advance suggested that the Marano could be reached swiftly, but it soon became clear that the Germans were determined to resist. At 1545hrs, BR 2nd Armoured Brigade attacked south of Coriano, soon clashing with the German line of defence running through the villages of San Clemente–San Savino–Croce and forming an arc south-east of Coriano to the east of Monte Colombo. Panzergrenadier-Regiment 71 from 29.Panzergrenadier-Division fiercely contested control of both Croce (east of Monte Colombo) and San Savino (south of Coriano), while German artillery relentlessly shelled the British armour, making full use of their observation posts at Gemmano. The BR 2nd Armoured Brigade had to pull back under cover of darkness after losing 55 of its 141 tanks, mostly to mechanical failure.

Belatedly, BR V Corps realized the importance of the Gemmano ridge, which directed the fire of at least 158 field, 56 medium and 14 heavy guns, along with 36 Nebelwerfer rocket launchers and 161 mortars. However, no plan had been laid down to seize the ridge, since BR 56th Division advanced across the

Fallschirmjäger firing an MG42 machine gun from a hasty position. Both the BR Eighth and US Fifth armies faced these soldiers once again, this time from 1.Fallschirmjäger-Division and 4.Fallschirmjäger-Division. (ullstein bild via Getty Images)

A captured soldier from the German 29.Panzer-Division, 7 September 1944. (© Imperial War Museum, NA 18403)

Conca towards Monte Colombo and IND 4th Division's advance was slowed down by the fierce resistance of 278.Infanterie-Division in the Tavolato–Pian Di Castello area. A breakthrough north towards Coriano would have resolved the situation, and on 5 September both BR 56th and 1st Armoured divisions attacked the German positions east and south of the line Monte Colombo–Coriano.

What followed was a fierce struggle that saw the tanks of BR 9th Lancers enter San Savino only to be driven away by 98.Infanterie-Division's troops, as a result of the tanks' lack of infantry support. San Savino was only secured under darkness, after the intervention of BR 18th Brigade. In the meantime, BR 56th Division brought forward two brigades to attack Croce, east of Monte Colombo, and pave the way for the advance of BR 7th Armoured Brigade. During the night of 6/7 September, control of Croce was contested, the town changing hands several times until the arrival of BR 7th Brigade's armour, which repelled a German counter-attack. To make things worse, BR 56th Division's 169th Brigade, held in reserve to attack Gemmano, was delayed by rain, and on the 7th its advance was halted by a counter-attack from Gebirgsjäger-Regiment 100.

On 6 September, as the rain started to pour down, turning the roads into quagmires, General Leese acknowledged that the first phase of Operation *Olive* had come to an end. After a major regrouping, he ordered a three-stage offensive: to the left, BR V Corps – with IND 4th, BR 46th, BR 56th and BR 1st Armoured divisions – was to attack Coriano using the last two divisions, while the former two secured the western flank. The CDN I Corps, with the CDN 5th Armoured and CDN 1st Infantry divisions, to be joined by the BR 4th Infantry and NZ 2nd divisions, was to continue its attacks against Coriano and along the coastal road. In the second phase, BR 4th Division was to move through CDN 5th Armoured Division's positions and advance across the Marano. The third and last phase was to see BR 4th Division along with the CDN 1st Division attack San Fortunato, south of Rimini, breaching the German defences.

While the fight for Croce and Gemmano continued, on 8 September BR 169th Brigade retook the village after a German counter-attack, but it failed to seize Gemmano. Delays in regrouping and the continuous rain postponed the start of the offensive from 10/11 to 12/13 September. General von Vietinghoff, visiting the front on 7 September, surely had reasons for concern about the incoming Allied attack. The 98.Infanterie-Division's infantry battalions were down to a strength of some 100 men each, while those of 29.Panzergrenadier-Division had an average strength of 250–300. Although Fallschirmjäger-Regiment 1 still had 862 men, Fallschirmjäger-Regiment 3 was down to 370 effectives and Fallschirmjäger-Regiment 4 to 153. Only 26.Panzer-Division's two Panzergrenadier battalions still had 788 and 503 men respectively.

At 1800hrs on 12 September, 700 guns started a five-hour (seven-hour in front of CDN I Corps) bombardment of the German positions at Coriano and the surrounding area. At night, the two infantry brigades of BR 1st Armoured Division stormed San Savino, driving through the boundary between 98.Infanterie-Division and 26.Panzer-Division. San Savino itself, defended by one battalion from 26.Panzer-Division and two from 98.Infanterie-Division, held until the afternoon on the 13th, when the German defenders finally surrendered, BR 1st Armoured Division taking 789 prisoners. The southern prong of the double thrust against Coriano ridge was followed at 0100hrs on the 13th by the attack of CDN 5th Armoured Division against the northern

end of the ridge, which the Canadians seized in the afternoon. The Germans held the town of Coriano until midday on the 14th, withdrawing that same afternoon. This enabled CDN 5th Armoured Division to rest and reorganize while being replaced by BR 4th Division, whose movement towards the front was slowed by rain and shelling.

A CDN 1st Armoured Division Churchill tank supports the advance towards the Gothic Line, near Fano, 26 August 1944. The initial successes in this area soon developed into vicious fighting in the Rimini area, 40km to the north-west. (© Imperial War Museum, NA 18050)

It soon became clear that the seizure of Coriano was not as significant as hoped, as BR Eighth Army faced yet another ridge. At 1700hrs on the 13th, BR 1st Armoured Division attacked the Ripabianca ridge just south of the Marano stream, still defended by the Germans on the reverse slope of Coriano. Its advance was halted by both a swollen stream and the German defences. The BR Eighth Army noticed how the German resistance stiffened continually, as proved by the fact that it lost, on average, 145 killed and 600 wounded every day. The problem was that BR V Corps, which was meant to be a pursuit formation, had failed to adopt the methodical advance required by the local terrain. As a result, on 14 September, BR 46th Division was ordered to hand control of Gemmano to IND 4th Division and to advance across the Conca toward Monte Colombo, while the BR 1st Armoured and 56th divisions were to clear the Ripabianca ridge.

On 14/15 September, BR 46th Division easily seized Monte Colombo and approached the southern end of the Marano as the Germans started to withdraw to the Rimini line, with IND 4th Division simultaneously clearing Gemmano. By the 17th, BR 46th Division had reached the border of the Republic of San Marino, while IND 4th Division was pulled out of the front line for rest. That same day, the BR 56th and 1st Armoured divisions cleared the Ripabianca ridge approaching the Marano. To their right the BR 4th and CDN 1st divisions made more rapid progress, crossing the Marano between 13 and 14 September, and establishing bridgeheads a day before both the BR 56th and 1st Armoured divisions did. The former faced German opposition until the 16th, just as the BR 4th and CDN 1st divisions did at San Fortunato ridge. Here, thanks to an Allied error (the Canadians evacuated the town of San Martino, and the Germans reoccupied it at once), the advance was slowed

The British commander-in-chief Harold Alexander inspects a Pantherturm position in early September 1944. These rare emplacements, if well positioned, could cover a wide area. (© Imperial War Museum, NA 18347)

just as 29.Panzergrenadier-Division withdrew in front of BR 4th Division.

Along the coast, GK 3rd Mountain Brigade, supported by NZ 2nd Division, was halted south of Rimini airfield, where a dug-in Panther turret proved to be very effective. This, and the German resistance at San Martino, slowed the Canadian advance, enabling new German units to deploy at the front. Indeed, this was a moment of crisis for Kesselring, who, on meeting Hitler on 5 September, was told to prepare for a withdrawal to the Alps, and for von Vietinghoff, who had just witnessed the freshly committed 356.Infanterie-Division being badly mauled immediately after its deployment at the front. Still, its arrival allowed the worn-out 71. and 98.Infanterie-Division to be relieved, while elements from 20.Luftwaffe-Feld-Division joined 1.Fallschirmjäger-Division as the final reserve unit – 90.Panzergrenadier-Division – began its deployment on the Rimini line. Meanwhile, on 16 September, General Leese ordered both corps to attack with infantry on a wide front in order to make the Germans spread their forces and to deal with the terrain, which rose sharply inland from the south-west of Rimini. The tanks were held in reserve and would be used in the pursuit.

On 17 September, everything was ready for the crossing of the Ausa stream and the attack towards the Rimini line. The BR 4th Division was the first to attack during the night of 17/18 September, supported by artificial light provided by searchlights reflecting off the clouds. This expedient surprised the Germans, who soon discovered they could not move or regroup their forces, which enabled the division to establish a bridgehead shortly after midnight. What followed was described as a battle of savage fury, the German resistance preventing BR 4th Division from reaching the western edge of the San Fortunato ridge. That same resistance prevented CDN 1st Division, deploying two Canadian and three New Zealand regiments moving under cover of a smokescreen, to cross the Ausa after attacking at 1600hrs on the 18th. Facing the 17 newly deployed 88mm guns from schwere Panzerjäger-Abteilung 590 (a heavy anti-tank battalion), supported by machine-gun fire, the Canadians were unable to cross the stream and withdrew. Within a matter of days, the successful German defence would prove to be transient.

On the 19th, BR 4th Division secured the bridgehead and brought the supporting tanks forward, while CDN 1st Division succeeded in crossing the Ausa and advanced to San Fortunato ridge, gaining a foothold on its south-eastern slopes. This enabled BR 4th Division to attack the same ridge and eventually dislodge the units from 1.Fallschirmjäger-Division and 29.Panzergrenadier-Division defending it, just as CDN 1st Division advanced with infantry supported by tanks. After bitter fighting, CDN 1st Division

Greek soldiers from the 3rd Mountain Brigade in street fighting on the outskirts of Rimini in September 1944. The brigade, which lacked battlefield experience, would soon be withdrawn and sent back to Greece. (Public Domain)

reached the main road to the north-west of the Ausa, only to face a German counter-attack. Having overcome the San Fortunato ridge defences, General Burns brought forward BR 1st Armoured Division, while the rest of CDN I Corps swung north-east, leaving the task of pursuing the German withdrawal from Rimini to GK 3rd Mountain Brigade.

On the left flank, BR V Corps faced a favourable situation. After 18/19 September, San Marino was reported to be undefended, just as BR 56th Division established a bridgehead on the Ausa, on the 19th both the 56th and 1st Armoured divisions clashed with 90.Panzergrenadier-Division, which had just relieved 356.Infanterie-Division in the area. Soon the British attack was halted on the German defences, which were supported by fire from 88mm guns. In the meantime, the BR 46th and IND 4th divisions secured the left flank, cleaning up the San Marino area.

On 20 September, the BR 4th and CDN 1st divisions advanced, reaching the Marecchia River, where they both established bridgeheads the following day. The German defences, including elements from 162.Infanterie-Division and 20.Luftwaffe-Feld-Division, simply disintegrated, leaving 29.Panzergrenadier-Division no other choice than to withdraw. By midday, von Vietinghoff realized the extent of the crisis and ordered a general fighting withdrawal to the Marecchia (the Adelheid Line), which was carried out that night. On 21 September, GK 3rd Mountain Brigade and supporting New Zealand tanks entered Rimini, and on the 22nd, two battalions were across the Marecchia. Heavy rain and exhaustion brought the offensive to a halt, while on the 23rd, both CDN 5th Armoured and NZ 2nd Division were brought forward for the next phase of the offensive.

Also on the 23rd, BR 46th and IND 4th divisions completed clearing San Marino at the cost of 36 casualties, while taking 54 German prisoners.[5] After a month of bitter and costly fighting, BR Eighth Army had reached its promised land.

---

5   San Marino was, and still is, an independent country and formally neutral. The Germans in fact only offered token resistance. On 23 September 1944, San Marino declared war on Germany.

US Fifth Army's assault on the Gothic Line, 1–22 September 1944

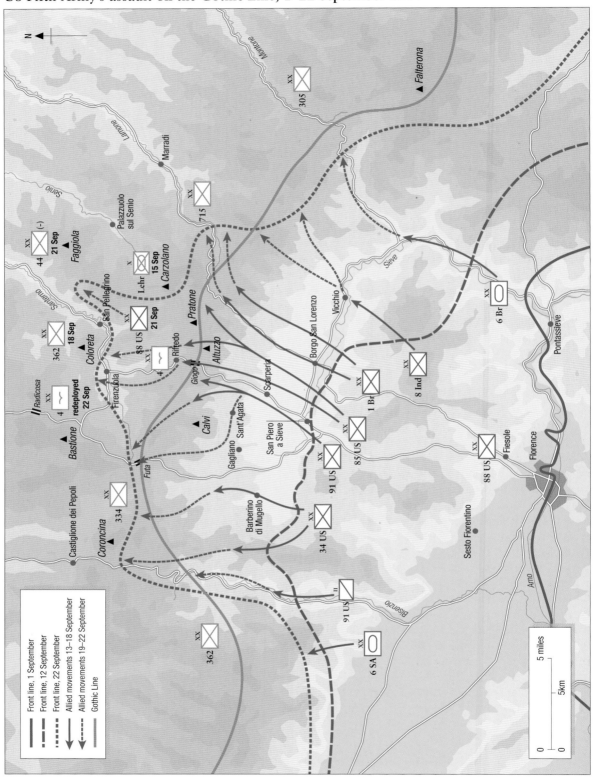

N

Mattione

▲ *Falterona*

XX 305

Lamone

● Marradi

Senio

XX 715

● Palazzuolo sul Senio

XX 44 (-) **21 Sep** ▲ *Faggiola*

Santerno

x L.chr **15 Sep** ▲ *Carzolano*

XX 362 **18 Sep** *Coloreta*

San Pellegrino

XX 88 US **21 Sep** ▲ *Pratone*

● Firenzuola

Riffedo ▲ *Altuzzo*

▲ *Radicosa* XX 4

XX 4 **redeployed 22 Sep**

Bastione Futa

Sieve

XX 6 Br

Vicchio ●

Borgo San Lorenzo ●

● Scarperia

▲ *Calvi*

Sant'Agata ●

Gagliano ●

San Piero a Sieve ●

XX 1 Br

XX 8 Ind

● Pontassieve

XX 85/US

XX 334 *Coroncina* ▲

Castiglione dei Pepoli ●

XX 91 US

Barberino di Mugello ●

XX 34 US

● Sesto Fiorentino

XX 88 US ● Fiesole

● Florence

Arno

II 91 US

Bisenzio

XX 6 SA

XX 362

Legend

▮▮▮	Front line, 1 September
┋┋┋	Front line, 12 September
┊┊┊	Front line, 22 September
→	Allied movements 13–18 September
⇢	Allied movements 19–22 September
━━	Gothic Line

5 miles
5km
0
0

46

US FIFTH ARMY PIERCES THE GOTHIC LINE

As BR Eighth Army started its offensive, US Fifth Army remained in the rest areas behind the front. One of the reasons for this was the need to wait for the re-opening of Leghorn harbour (seized on 19 July) on 3 September, since this was to be the new main source of supply for the army. Another reason was the need to await Alexander's order to attack.

In the meantime, General Clark developed his attack plan. The idea was to push US II Corps forward by about 10km to the Sieve River, the first phase of the offensive, while US IV Corps simulated the crossing of the Arno River. Of the two passes leading north across the Apennines, the Futa was clearly the most heavily defended, so the main weight of the American attack was to fall on the more lightly defended Giogo Pass. From there it would be possible to outflank the Futa Pass from Firenzuola and complete the breakthrough of the Gothic Line.

The German withdrawal, which began on 29 August, rendered the first phase of Clark's plan unnecessary. On 31 August, the US IV and II corps began to advance, the former with orders to cross the Arno, which its patrols found undefended. That same day, General Crittenberger had the US 1st Armored Division, supported by 370th RCT of US 92nd Division, cross the river followed by SA 6th Armoured Division and TF 45. Only on 4 September, after reaching the main road from Florence, did US IV Corps' units start to encounter some German resistance. This, and the rain that started falling the next day, convinced Crittenberger not to move beyond the objectives he had been given; thus, he ordered his units to regroup and to consolidate the line running from the Serchio River valley to Lucca. On 10 September, TF 45 seized the seaside resort of Viareggio as the SA 6th Division entered Pistoia. Meanwhile, BR XIII Corps also went in pursuit of the withdrawing German forces, advancing between 6km and 15km north of the Arno.

German destruction made the mountain roads even more difficult to negotiate for the advancing American troops, as clearly shown here. (NARA)

US II Corps' advance saw US 91st Division move along the road leading to the Giogo Pass, while to the left the US 34th Division advanced along the main Route 65 towards the Futa Pass, its left flank secured by US 91st Cavalry Reconnaissance Squadron. Both divisions, which had been ready to advance to the Gothic Line defences since 7 September, waited until the 10th, when Field Marshal Alexander eventually gave the order. On that day, US II Corps moved forward on a 25km-wide front reaching the Sieve River and crossing it, before facing its first serious German resistance the following day.

General Lemelsen's AOK 14, withdrawing to the Green Line defences, was considerably weakened, having already ceded three of its divisions to AOK

The winding road leading to the Giogo Pass, at the top of the photo. The nature of the terrain required the use of infantry, and prevented armour from being deployed. (US Army)

10 for the defence of the Rimini area. As a consequence, I.Fallschirm-Korps' units were compelled to extend the portions of the line they had been defending, in particular 4.Fallschirmjäger-Division, which was now defending both the Futa and the Giogo passes. Faced not only with the American advance but also with the Italian Partisan threat and the constant air attacks on its lines of communication, AOK 14 had practically no reserves, apart from the weak Grenadier-Lehr-Brigade. Hence, on 9 September, Lemelsen asked Kesselring to deploy at least one of the worn-out divisions that had been pulled out of AOK 10's line in his area. Kesselring agreed, although he saw no reason for immediate concern in AOK 14's zone of operation.

On 12 September, US 91st Infantry Division's 363rd RCT led the advance to the Giogo Pass, with US 85th Division ordered forward to support the attack. The apparent lack of German defences led Colonel Magill, the regimental commander, to send I./363rd with one company from III./363rd against the dominating features of Monte Monticelli and one company from III./363rd against Monte Altuzzo, hoping for their swift seizure. Both struggled with the unfamiliar terrain and the German defence, which compelled them to halt their advance before reaching their objectives. The company from III./363rd sent against Altuzzo became lost and was unable to make contact with the advancing US 85th Division's 338th RCT the following day.

The German defences, mostly dug into the rock and protected by barbed-wire obstacles, fully exploited the terrain, with Monte Monticelli dominating the Giogo Pass (itself well defended) on the west, while Monte Altuzzo dominated it from the east. Not only were the German defences solid, but, as the GIs were soon to discover, they were also hard to detect while moving through rocky terrain with plenty of gullies and ravines, the features of which were completely unknown. The only advantage was that, in most cases, this kind of terrain permitted an approach by stealth.

On 13 September, I./363rd RCT attacked Monticelli, followed on its right flank by II./363rd; both were compelled to halt by enemy fire. It was soon clear that the terrain would only permit attacks by small groups, and that artillery support was necessary. On the 14th, both I./363rd and II./363rd's companies attacked one section at a time after a rolling artillery barrage, but were halted once again by the German defences. When darkness fell, the two battalions managed to infiltrate the defences and approach the top of the mountain, repelling a German counter-attack thanks to the intervention of artillery. On the morning of 15 September, 363rd RCT's attack was renewed to exploit the advance, again facing German counter-attacks that continued until the following day. That same afternoon, III./363rd RCT was committed to the right flank, but its advance was soon disrupted by enemy fire. After

a rolling artillery barrage, the three battalions of 363rd RCT launched a massive attack on the 17th, which led them to the crest of the mountain by mid-afternoon. Once again, the Germans counter-attacked.

Since Company C of 363rd RCT's position at Monte Altuzzo was unknown, on 13 September US 85th Division's 338th RCT advanced without artillery cover. To the left, II./338th RCT was sent along the main road, while in the centre I./338th RCT moved towards Altuzzo (without making contact with C./363rd RCT). The divisional right flank was secured by 339th RCT, which approached Monte Verruca, but was slowed by fire coming from Altuzzo. On that day, US II Corps' artillery began a 24-hour artillery harassing fire, aimed at preventing the Germans from shifting forces or bringing in reinforcements. On the 14th, while II./338th RCT's advance along the road was halted by the German defences and by the fire coming from Monticelli and Altuzzo, Company B from 338th RCT advanced to the eastern ridge of Monte Altuzzo, reaching the German main line of defence, just as Company A was forced to withdraw.

On the 15th, as the US 85th Division committed its 337th RCT to the right flank in support of the 339th in the advance towards Monte Verruca, companies A and C, 338th RCT advanced on the eastern ridge of Monte Altuzzo, repelling the German counter-attacks. At this point, all the reserves available to AOK 14 – I.Fallschirm-Korps and 4.Fallschirmjäger-Division –

US FIFTH ARMY SEIZES MONTE ALTUZZO, 13–17 SEPTEMBER 1944

With the Germans waiting for the enemy main effort at the trans-Appenine Futa Pass, US II Corps directed its attack towards the Giogo Pass instead. Preceded by the units of US 91st Division, which approached Monte Altuzzo, US 85th Division deployed its 338th RCT to seize the 926m-high Monte Altuzzo and the Giogo Pass in order to open the way for the Allied advance northwards. The area, defended by the men of Fallschirmjäger-Regiment 12 subsequently reinforced by elements from the Grenadier-Lehr-Brigade, soon witnessed a major battle fought in challenging terrain.

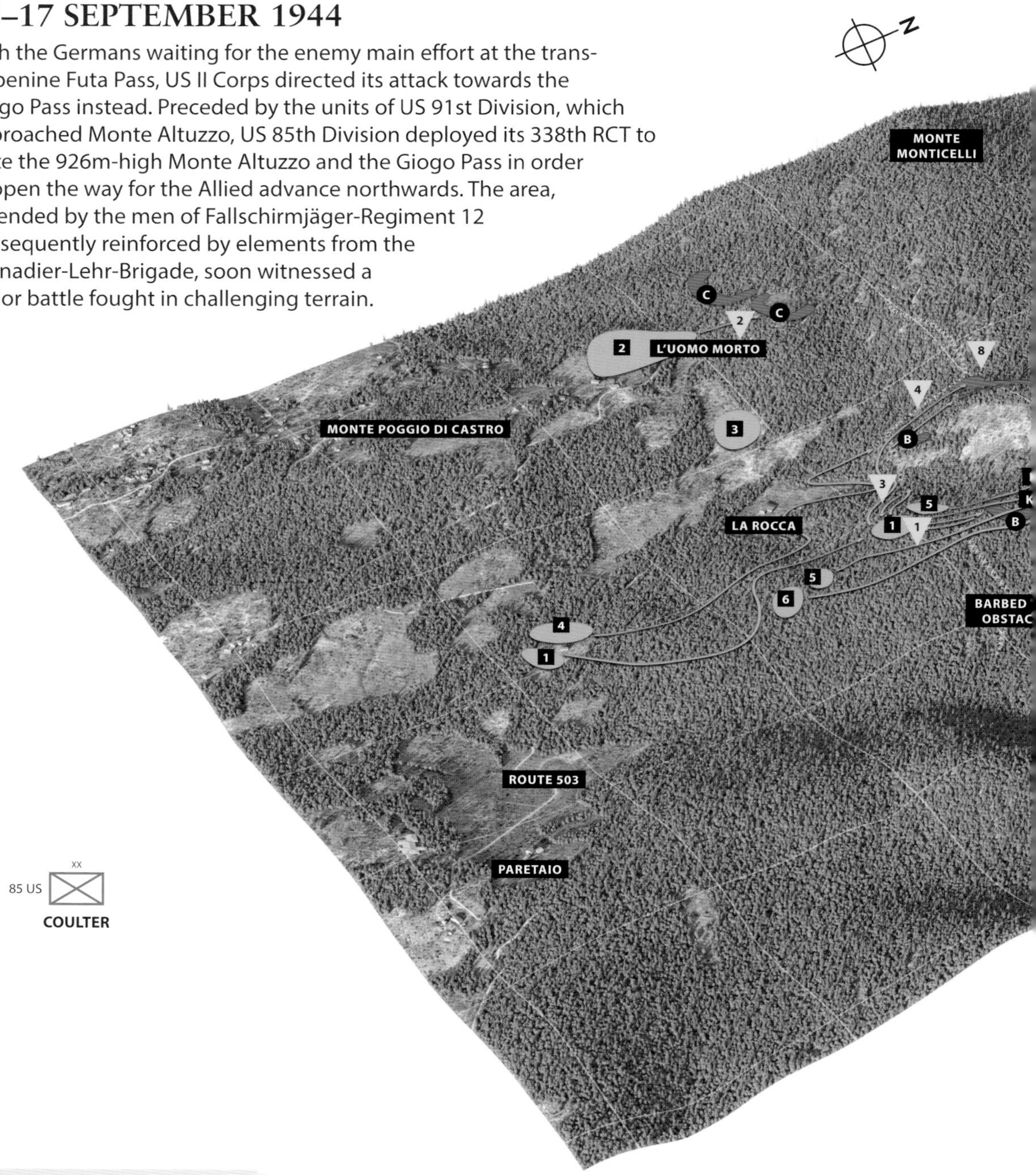

MONTE MONTICELLI

L'UOMO MORTO

MONTE POGGIO DI CASTRO

LA ROCCA

BARBED OBSTAC

ROUTE 503

PARETAIO

85 US | XX |

COULTER

ALLIED
US 338th RCT, US 85th Infantry Division:
1. A./338th RCT
2. II./338th RCT
3. E./338th RCT
4. B./338th RCT
5. C./338th RCT
6. III./338th RCT

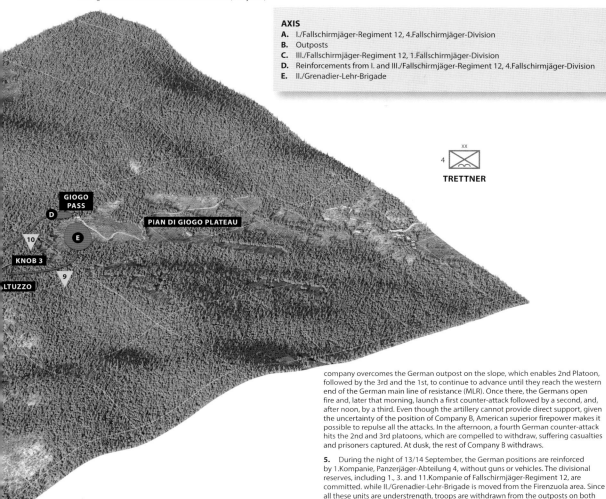

Note: gridlines are shown at intervals of 500m (547 yards)

AXIS

A. I./Fallschirmjäger-Regiment 12, 4.Fallschirmjäger-Division
B. Outposts
C. III./Fallschirmjäger-Regiment 12, 1.Fallschirmjäger-Division
D. Reinforcements from I. and III./Fallschirmjäger-Regiment 12, 4.Fallschirmjäger-Division
E. II./Grenadier-Lehr-Brigade

XX
4
TRETTNER

GIOGO
PASS

D

PIAN DI GIOGO PLATEAU

E

10

KNOB 3

9

LTUZZO

company overcomes the German outpost on the slope, which enables 2nd Platoon, followed by the 3rd and the 1st, to continue to advance until they reach the western end of the German main line of resistance (MLR). Once there, the Germans open fire and, later that morning, launch a first counter-attack followed by a second, and, after noon, by a third. Even though the artillery cannot provide direct support, given the uncertainty of the position of Company B, American superior firepower makes it possible to repulse all the attacks. In the afternoon, a fourth German counter-attack hits the 2nd and 3rd platoons, which are compelled to withdraw, suffering casualties and prisoners captured. At dusk, the rest of Company B withdraws.

5. During the night of 13/14 September, the German positions are reinforced by 1.Kompanie, Panzerjäger-Abteilung 4, without guns or vehicles. The divisional reserves, including 1., 3. and 11.Kompanie of Fallschirmjäger-Regiment 12, are committed. while II./Grenadier-Lehr-Brigade is moved from the Firenzuola area. Since all these units are understrength, troops are withdrawn from the outposts on both sides of the MLR.

15 September

6. Having been on the move since 0300hrs, Company C, US 338th RCT makes contact with Company A near Hill 782, which is attacked at 0900hrs. After overcoming the German defenders, the two companies move past Knob 1 and make contact with the eastern end of the German MLR at Knob 2. Both companies A and C are counter-attacked by the Germans, but the latter are once again driven back thanks to superior American firepower.

16–17 September

7. At 1030hrs on the 16th, Company C attacks towards knobs 1 and 2, while Company A moves towards the western ridge. As the German resistance begins to crack, Company C succeeds in reaching Knob 1 only to halt because of the friendly artillery fire directed against the German positions and the darkness. During the night, 3rd Platoon of Company C reaches Knob 2 and manages to drive back the German defenders, thus paving the way for the advance to Monte Altuzzo's summit, Hill 926. At about 0300hrs on the 17th, the 3rd Platoon of Company C resumes its advance, followed by 2nd Platoon and the rest of Company C, which deploys on Monte Altuzzo. At the same time, III./US 338th RCT takes up position between Hill 782 and the southern slope of Hill 926.

8. At dusk 1st Platoon, Company A approaches the western ridge, where the men dig in and await dawn. By mid-morning, the platoon has secured the summit.

9. Deploying under American artillery fire, II./Grenadier-Lehr-Brigade reaches the northern slopes of Monte Altuzzo. It will counter-attack Company C's positions several times from 1000hrs on the 17th, without success.

10. In the afternoon of 17 September, Company K, US 338th RCT moves from its positions to the south of Hill 926, reaching Knob 3. Counter-attacks from II./Grenadier-Lehr-Brigade eventually compel Company K to withdraw, but in the evening the Germans decide to abandon their positions and start their withdrawal to the north at dusk, leaving Monte Altuzzo in American hands.

▼ **EVENTS**

13 September

1. On 12 September, the approach to Monte Altuzzo of Company L, US 363rd RCT of US 91st Infantry Division is halted by friendly artillery fire and uncertainty about its own position. US 85th Infantry Division's 338th RCT takes over and deploys during the night of 12/13 September, with the 2nd Battalion moving on to Hill 770 along the main road, the 1st Battalion attacking Monte Altuzzo and the 3rd Battalion held in reserve. At dawn on the 13th, 3rd and 1st platoons, Company A, US 338th RCT advance, reaching Hill 664 by noon. Any further advance to Hill 782 is halted by fire from a German outpost. Eventually, the company withdraws at night. The 2nd Platoon advances towards the western German outposts before turning back via La Rocca farmhouse. Company A deploys for defence.

2. The attack by II./US 338th RCT is halted by German mortar and machine-gun fire and a lack of US artillery support. Another attack takes place at noon on 16 September, but again it fails to break through the German defences.

14 September

3. While artillery fire pounds the German positions, Company A, US 338th RCT attacks Hill 782 head on, being halted at first by the barbed wire, then clashing with a German bunker dug into the rock. Barbed wire and German machine-gun fire prevent any US advance, and the company eventually withdraws.

4. During the night of 13/14 September, Company B, US 338th RCT reaches the slopes of Hill 624, and locates a trail that leads it to the southern slope of Hill 782 at 0025hrs on the 14th. From there the company swings to the left, reaching the south-western slopes of Monte Altuzzo. At dawn, with 2nd Platoon in the lead, the

Shown here is the reason why the US Fifth Army resorted to Italian-manned mule pack companies: a 2½-ton truck has overturned on a mountain road near the Giogo Pass. (US Army)

were committed to the front, including elements from 10.Fallschirmjäger-Regiment pulled out from the Futa Pass, anti-tank and replacement units, plus elements from 305.Infanterie-Division and the two-battalion-strong Grenadier-Lehr-Brigade, all reaching the area on 16/17 September. However, this was too late, because over the space of these two days, the American attacks made decisive progress. On the morning of the 17th, elements of I./338th RCT reached the peak of Monte Altuzzo, shortly before US 91st Division's 363rd RCT seized the crest of Monte Monticelli; later that day, it took Monte Verruca along with the nearby Monte Pratone. The Germans promptly counter-attacked, in particular at Monte Altuzzo, where elements from the Grenadier-Lehr-Brigade were committed and practically annihilated. Faced with the reality of the situation, General Lemelsen ordered I.Fallschirm-Korps to abandon the Green I line and withdraw north to Green II, north of Firenzuola. The withdrawal started that same night.

In less than a week, US II Corps had broken through the Gothic Line, which left General Clark with a strategic choice to make. Given the latest developments, the corps had two main options: continue to advance north along the main road (Route 65) from Florence to the Futa Pass–Radicosa Pass towards Bologna, or switch east in the direction of Imola to strike at the boundary between AOK 14 and AOK 10, which meant supporting BR Eighth Army's offensive at the same time. This key moment saw Clark make a half-hearted choice, which in all likelihood undermined future US II Corps operations. The bulk of the corps, with the US 34th, 91st and 85th divisions, was to continue the attack towards Bologna, while US 88th Division was committed to the east, towards Imola.

A 2½-ton truck crossing a Bailey bridge at Porretta Terme – 50km south-west of Bologna. These bridges proved essential in maintaining the Allied flow of supplies to the front. (PhotoQuest/Getty Images)

Terrain had a decisive influence on the decision. Logistically, only Route 65 was adequate to support the main effort. The road passing through the Giogo Pass to Firenzuola and Imola was a single-track mountain road unable to support any great logistic effort, and pack animals were often used to bring supplies to the front. Facing the German withdrawal and the outflanking of the Gothic Line defences, US 85th Division advanced toward Firenzuola, which was reached on the 21st, just as the US 88th Division was brought forward. To the left US 91st Division, with one regiment already advancing toward the Futa Pass, was able to outflank its defences from the east. On the 22nd, its 362nd RCT seized the pass, opening the way to the advance towards Bologna.

An M7 'Priest' SP gun fires its 105mm howitzer at German positions in the Apennines in mid-September 1944. The intense use of artillery against German positions was essential in breaching the Gothic Line defences. (US Army)

BR EIGHTH ARMY'S OFFENSIVE ON THE ROMAGNA PLAIN

The crossing of the Marecchia River in pouring rain on 21 September effectively brought to an end Operation *Olive*, as this marked the conclusion of the fighting in broken countryside and sanctioned BR Eighth Army's access to the flat terrain of Romagna. This, it was hoped, would lead to a swift breakthrough of the German defences, as had happened with the Gothic Line during the previous month. There were, however, a series of factors mitigating against this. The terrain was the most problematic. It was soon discovered that the Romagna plain was unsuitable for tanks. The lack of observation points made the use of artillery difficult, while the many rivers, streams and irrigation ditches, almost entirely running west to east, presented formidable obstacles. Most of these, in particular the irrigation ditches, had flood banks standing 15–30m above the fields, suitable for defence but not for attack. When not used for defence, the banks were destroyed by the Germans, flooding the fields and making them impassable for tanks. Heavy rains contributed to the flooding, and the weather greatly impeded air observation and support. Moreover, the countryside was littered with small farms and villages that were soon turned into strongpoints by the Germans, which once again required the use of Allied infantry.

Unfortunately, BR Eighth Army had suffered heavy casualties, particularly in its infantry units, during the first stage of the offensive. The solutions employed, like the disbanding of BR 1st Armoured Division and the conversion to infantry of anti-aircraft units, soon proved insufficient. With casualties amounting to 529 officers and 7,147 other ranks among infantry alone, out of a total of 14,000 from 24 August to 21 September, BR Eighth Army was suffering from both attrition and the German determination to resist. Its main opponent LXXVI.Panzer-Korps took some 16,000 casualties, which is about half the total losses suffered by Heeresgruppe C in September (30,251). Also, tank losses were considerable; during the same period BR Eighth Army saw a total of 130 Shermans, 60 Churchills and 20 Stuart tanks written off against German losses of 100 tanks and 124 anti-tank and self-propelled guns.

Fallschirmjäger riding a battered motorcycle with sidecar warily watch for enemy aircraft. Allied air superiority and artillery fire greatly hampered German troop movements. (ullstein bild via Getty Images)

Unsurprisingly, General Leese's aim was to exploit the situation with a swift advance along the main routes: the coastal Via Adriatica route to Ravenna and Ferrara, and the inland Via Emilia to Forlì and Bologna. The Via Adriatica was the first target discussed on 16 September among the corps commanders, Leese having CDN I Corps with NZ 2nd Infantry, CDN 5th Armoured and BR 1st Armoured deployed to attack along the coast while BR V Corps regrouped. At the same time, the Desert Air Force started a bombing campaign against the Savio River bridges, which did not completely interrupt communications in the area thanks to the skills of the German engineers.

On 26/27 September, the new phase of the offensive started with NZ 2nd Division crossing the Uso River – the new German defensive line – without difficulty, having crossed the Marecchia on the 21st, its 4th Brigade making slow progress against the German rearguards. The NZ 5th Brigade, which moved through CDN 1st Division, encountered little resistance from the remnants of a *Kampfgruppe* formed from 162.Infanterie-Division and elements of 1.Fallschirmjäger-Division. On 27/28 September, NZ 2nd Division elements reached the Rubicone (or Rubicon, also known as the Fiumicino) River, as the GK 3rd Mountain Brigade supported its advance on the west side of the road. The CDN 5th Armoured Division's 5th Armoured Brigade also advanced rapidly across the Uso, reaching the Rubicone on the 28th, but an attempt to establish a bridgehead ended badly when the rain prevented reinforcements from reaching the Irish Regiment across the river, with the result that a 26.Panzer-Division counter-attack wiped it out.

In the meantime, BR V Corps also continued its advance. After a hard fight to cross the Marecchia on 22 and 23 September, on the 24th, BR 1st Armoured Division fought its last action, opening the way through Santarcangelo before being relieved by BR 56th Division. Also on that same day, the BR 46th and IND 4th divisions secured their bridgeheads on the Marecchia, facing counter-attacks from the newly arrived 114.Jäger and 278. Infanterie-Division. The IND 4th Division was then replaced on 3 October by IND 10th Division, before being earmarked for transfer to Greece.

Relying on BR 1st Armoured Division's bridgehead, BR 56th Division crossed both the Marecchia and the Uso, advancing straight to Savignano. Its leading 169th Brigade had to face determined resistance from elements of 90.Panzergrenadier-Division that eventually forced the evacuation of the modest bridgehead on the Rubicone, leading to the capture of the soldiers at Savignano. Rain prevented another attack from being launched that aimed to establish a solid bridgehead. The German defence on the Rubicone prevented both BR 46th and IND 4th divisions from crossing the river, as the supply situation became critical. The rain had made roads and rivers impassable, and a Bailey bridge on the Uso was washed away. Allied activity shrank to patrolling, which reported that the west bank of the Rubicone was well defended, as the skeletal BR X Corps followed the German withdrawal to Green Line II, about 25km north of Cesena.

As US 88th Infantry Division advanced along the route towards Imola, BR Eighth Army's predicament changed. On 25 September, Leese, considering that German resistance was more likely than a general withdrawal, decided to regroup his forces in order to prepare to force the German defensive line with both CDN I and BR V corps, plus POL II Corps deployed inland. While the Polish redeployment was, once again, slowed down by the weather, on 1 October Leese was replaced by General McCreery, who had his own views on the tactical situation. Facing an infantry manpower crisis, which led to the disbanding of BR 1st Armoured Division and the reorganization of the infantry battalions into three companies, McCreery had to face the fact that hopes of reaching the Po River were vanishing. On 22 September, the idea of a landing in Istria was discussed. On 3 October, the Po Task Force was disbanded. Realizing that the situation could only worsen (and after the ammunition crisis began to manifest itself in mid-October, on the 23rd Alexander announced the redeployment to Greece of GK 3rd Mountain Brigade and IND 4th Division), McCreery made his own, minor changes to Leese's plan.

The idea was to switch to BR X and POL II corps, which only faced the German 305.Infanterie-Division. At the same time, the advance along the coastal route was to become secondary, as both CDN I and BR V Corps were to press on along the Via Emilia towards Bologna on the left flank. The planned crossing of the Rubicone on 1/2 and 5/6 October was cancelled

A patrol from the BR 7th Oxford and Bucks Regiment, BR 56th Division, pauses during a reconnaissance mission near the German strongpoint of Gemmano, 20km south of Rimini, on 6 September 1944. Infantry played a major role throughout the entire Gothic Line campaign, and suffered accordingly. (© Imperial War Museum, NA 18394)

An 88mm PAK 43 anti-tank gun, the ground version of the dual-purpose weapon, in an emplacement on the outskirts of Rimini, 22 September 1943. (Bundesarchiv, Bild 101I-315-1127-03/Lüthge/CC-BY-SA 3.0)

A StuG III destroyed by POL II Corps in the Gothic Line fighting. (Public Domain)

because of heavy rain, and NZ 2nd Division was replaced by the ad hoc Cumberland Force, the latter put together by the HQ of CDN 5th Armoured Brigade (of which Brigadier Cumberland was the CO) under the command of Wilderforce, itself made up of the NZ Cavalry Regiment plus GK 3rd Mountain Brigade along with dismounted Canadian units. The NZ 2nd Division could then redeploy to the right flank of CDN 1st Infantry Division.

Before CDN I and BR V corps started their offensives, on 6 October IND 10th Division crossed the Rubicone. The next day, it seized a key feature just as the BR 46th Division was also crossing the river, and both faced German counter-attacks. Since 29 September, the Germans had been withdrawing from the Rubicone to the Pisciatello River, although in indescribable conditions of chaos, rain and enemy shelling. Facing the new threat to its right wing, on 9 October von Vietinghoff authorized LXXVI. Panzer-Korps to begin a fighting withdrawal back to the Senio, which would slow the enemy advance and make the Allies pay for every inch of ground.

This actually enabled both NZ 2nd Division (with one brigade in the lead) and CDN 1st Division (with two brigades) to cross the Rubicone on 11 October (their way paved by BR 56th Division's seizure of Savignano), and make good progress north of the Via Emilia. The pace of their advance increased as they approached the Pisciatello River on the 14th, just as LXXVI. Panzer-Korps sped up its withdrawal to the Senio, which was completed four days later. Both the New Zealand and the Canadian troops reached the Pisciatello on the 17th, entering Cesena and establishing bridgeheads on 18/19 October; they faced no German opposition. The last leg of the advance to the Senio saw stiff opposition from LXXVI.Panzer-Korps rearguards. In the meantime, the IND 10th Division advance enabled BR

A Staghound armoured car from NZ 2nd Division's cavalry unit moving through the ruins of San Giorgio de Cesena, 21 October 1944. (Public Domain)

46th Division to progress across the Pisciatello to the Senio and Cesena, where, on 10/11 October, BR 4th Division was called up again, deploying on the 20th.

The first to cross the Savio on 20 October was BR 4th Division, even though its bridgehead could not be enlarged and had therefore to be abandoned. The next day, as Cumberland Force reached Cesenatico, IND 10th Division successfully crossed the river, taking advantage of 305.Infanterie-Division's over-stretched line of defence. At the same time, the division also faced serious supply problems. At this point, given the need to create an operational reserve, BR 46th Division was pulled out of the line along with NZ 2nd Division and CDN 5th Armoured Brigade, whose Cumberland Force was replaced by Porterforce, which was made up of British and Canadian dismounted units.

The real issue was that British commanders were now contemplating what to do next. Having realized that a breakthrough was no longer possible, Field Marshal Alexander determined that BR Eighth Army's operations should end by 15 November. General McCreery thought that 15 December was an appropriate deadline, even though progress was slow. The POL II Corps' deployment was impeded by difficult terrain, which meant that POL 5th Kresowa Division could only deploy on 17/18 October, and begin its advance the next day. Even though it was facing the weak 305.Infanterie-Division, the Polish division made limited progress, seizing Monte Colombo on the 23rd; this paved the way for the arrival at the front two days later of POL 3rd Carpathian Division, which then started to advance north along the Ronco River valley.

On 21/22 October, CDN 1st Division crossed the Savio north of Cesena, facing German counter-attacks and problems such as the Bailey bridge being swept away on the 26th, a day after it was laid down. Only IND 10th Division made progress, while BR 4th Division was halted at Cesena. This did not matter until 23 October, when LXXVI.Panzer-Korps started to withdraw again, this time to try to extricate 1.Fallschirmjäger-Division from the front, which was needed to face the threat posed by US Fifth Army. The withdrawal, which created a gap between 278.Infanterie-Division and 26.Panzer-Division, was successful, and by the 25th the Germans were on the Gudrun Line along the Ronco River. This facilitated the Allied advance. Facing little opposition, BR 4th Division moved along the Via Emilia, reaching Forlimpopoli on the 25th as IND 10th Division approached the Ronco and prepared to make contact with POL 3rd Division. Between 25 and 26 October, both IND 10th Division and BR 4th Division crossed the Ronco, the former successfully establishing a bridgehead at Meldola while the latter faced some difficulties. After a tank was hit and blocked a ford, BR 4th Division's small bridgehead was wiped out by a counter-attack from 278.Infanterie-Division, the reaction of which prevented the creation of a bridgehead on two further separate occasions.

Sergeant Galen Schmidt (standing beside the transit) and Corporal Jerome B. Petrie of the 39th Combat Engineers, US Fifth Army, surveying the terrain near the Futa Pass in front of an anti-tank ditch. (PhotoQuest/Getty Images)

The Allied two-pronged offensive, 22 September–1 November 1944

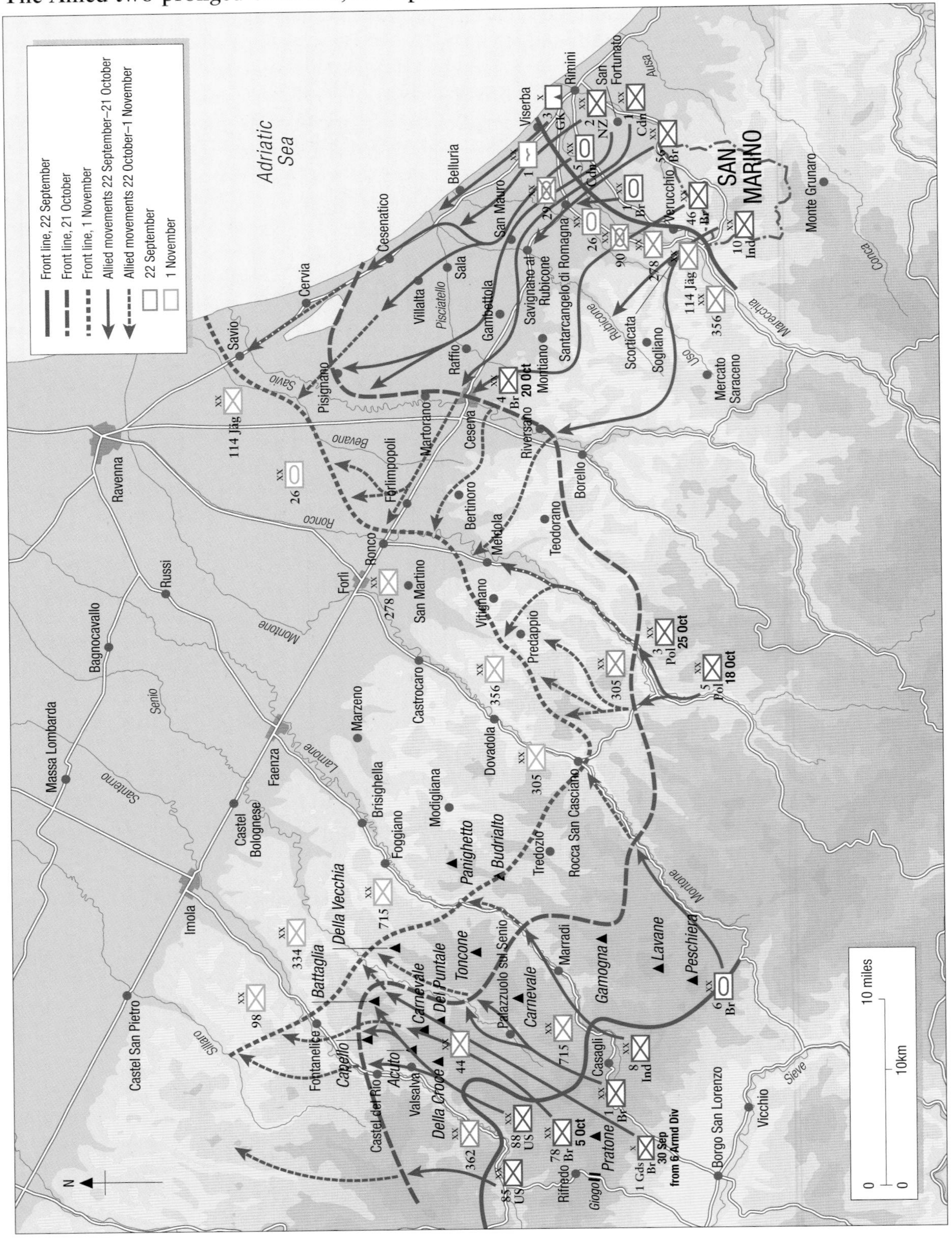

Legend:
- Front line, 22 September
- Front line, 21 October
- Front line, 1 November
- Allied movements 22 September–21 October
- Allied movements 22 October–1 November
- 22 September
- 1 November

Adriatic Sea

Rimini
San Fortunato
Viserba
Viserba
SAN MARINO
Monte Grunaro
Belluria
San Mauro
Cesenatico
Verucchio
Savignano di Romagna
Santarcangelo di Romagna
Cervia
Villalta
Pisciatello
Sala
Gambettola
Scorticata
Sogliano
Mercato Saraceno
Savio
Raffio
Pisignano
Mortiano
Martorano
Cesena
Riversano
Borello
Teodorano
Montiano
114 jäg **20 Oct**
4 Br
Ravenna
Forlimpopoli
Bertinoro
Mèldola
Forlì
Ronco
Ronco
Bevano
Russi
278
San Martino
Vitignano
Predappio
Bagnocavallo
San Martino
356
305
3 Pol **25 Oct**
Massa Lombarda
Marzeno
Castrocaro
Dovadola
305
5 Pol **18 Oct**
Faenza
Brisighella
Foggiano
Modigliana
Tredozio
Rocca San Casciano
Castel Bolognese
Della Vecchia
Panighetto
Budrialto
Marradi
Lavane
Peschiera
Gamogna
Imola
715
Battaglia
Toncone
Del Puntale
Carnevale
Palazzuolo sul Senio
Carnevale
715
6 Br
334
Castel San Pietro
98
Capello
Carnevale
Casaglia
8 Ind
362
Fontanelice
44
Valsalva
Della Croce
Alcuto
85 US
88 US
78 Br
Rifredo
Giogo II
Pratone
1 Gds Br
1 Br
Borgo San Lorenzo
Vicchio
Castel del Rio
5 Oct
30 Sep from 6 Armd Div
Sieve

N

10 miles
10km

58

On 26 October, as the Via Emilia became impassable following the collapse of a Bailey bridge, a temporary halt to operations was called just as POL 3rd Division made contact with IND 10th Division, the Poles seizing the town of Predappio (the birthplace of Benito Mussolini) the following day. The Canadian corps was relieved, while BR 46th Division replaced IND 10th Division. The task of reaching the Po now seemed to rest entirely on the shoulders of US Fifth Army.

THE THRUST TOWARDS IMOLA

After assembling, on 21 September, US 88th Infantry Division started its advance on a narrow mountain road, flanked by steep mountains, running along the Santerno River valley. The division, advancing on a 5km front which was to widen once the Po valley was reached, had the most important road junction in its path at Castel del Rio. The divisional commander, General Kendall, sent the 350th and 349th RCTs ahead to outflank the place, which was to be attacked by the 351st RCT. The advance was not without problems, as a German patrol, exploiting the thinly stretched American lines, was able to infiltrate and capture one battalion command post.

On the 23rd, Monte della Croce was seized, clearing the way for an attack on Monte Acuto the following day. The latter was seized on the 26th by 350th RCT, which continued its advance by also seizing the nearby Monte del Puntale. This facilitated contact with the neighbouring BR 1st Infantry Division, while to the west 349th RCT seized Monte Pratolungo, which dominated Castel del Rio. This compelled the Germans to abandon Castel del Rio, which was taken without a fight also on the 26th by 351st RCT. Facing the unexpected American advance, Kesselring reinforced the area with elements from LI.Gebirgs-Korps, with 715.Infanterie-Division deployed followed by 362.Infanterie-Division.

The German reaction was not only belated but also unsuccessful, since on 27 September II./350th RCT seized Monte Carnevale (the northernmost peak with the same name) by surprise, proceeding then towards Monte Battaglia. En route, II./350th encountered a group of Italian partisans, which guided it to the top of the undefended Monte Battaglia by mid-afternoon. The 44.Infanterie-Division, which now only held the peak of Monte Capello north-west of Monte Battaglia, counter-attacked at once, but II./350th was able to repulse two German night-time counter-attacks. Sensing the possibility of a breakthrough, General Kendall deployed 350th RCT ahead of the division, dispatching battalions to the tops of both mounts Carnevale and Battaglia, while 351st RCT was still at Castel del Rio. However, the regiment had stalled, since it was not able to drive the Germans away from Monte Capello, which also slowed the pace of advance of 349th RCT to the left. In order to fill the gap with BR 1st Infantry Division, dismounted tank crews had to be used as infantry while US 88th Division swung north. By the 27th, the entire CCA of US 1st Armored Division was deployed on its right flank.

Only II./350th was atop Monte Battaglia, the two other battalions being used to keep the road leading to the peak open and to secure communications, especially for stretcher-bearers who had to carry the wounded down the valley. This was also a necessity given the terrain, as the top of Monte

Men from the US 88th Division marching on a mountain road in September 1944. (PhotoQuest/Getty Images)

Battaglia offered no other cover than the ruins of a monastery, and was open to continuous enemy fire. While the Germans fired an average of 200–400 shells against the peak, American artillery replied with an average of 3,400 shells against the German positions. German counter-attacks soon materialized once again; on 28 September, a German counter-attack led to a desperate situation, stabilized only thanks to the arrival, at the top of the mountain, of a company from another battalion, which enabled them to repulse the counter-attack by 1700hrs. Faced with this situation, General Kendall committed the two other battalions of 350th RCT to the top of Monte Battaglia.

The next day, fighting continued in what had become an epic struggle. A new German counter-attack penetrated II./350th's perimeter, reaching the monastery ruins, but once again it was eventually repulsed. The seizure of Monte Capello by 351st RCT that same day eased the situation, as did BR 1st Division's advance on the right flank of US 88th Division. On 1 October, the Germans again stormed Monte Battaglia, and once more they were driven back by II./350th, which would be relieved that same day. The US 88th Division had come out on top, but its efforts had been in vain.

Facing the German resistance and the inadequate road, which was unable to support an entire division, General Clark decided to abandon the secondary thrust towards Imola, focusing instead on the drive towards Bologna along Route 65. As a consequence, US 88th Division's area was to be handed over to BR XIII Corps, and the division was to swing north on the right flank of US 85th Division. The US 350th RCT was to be relieved from 1 October by BR 1st Guards Brigade detached from BR 6th Armoured Division; the two other regiments would be relieved by the newly arrived BR 78th Division. The relief was completed in three days, and by 5 October US 88th Division was attacking north to the Sillaro River valley just as US 85th Division advanced along the Idice River valley. The cost for US 88th Division had been high: a total of 2,105 casualties, which is more than the entire US II Corps suffered while breaking through the Gothic Line.

The BR XIII Corps' progress had been even slower than that of US 88th Division. On 12/13 September, BR 1st Division advanced towards the Casaglia Pass, securing the heights commanding the road by the 15th. In the meantime, IND 8th Division, attacking mostly at night, overcame the defences of Grenadier-Regiment 725, also approaching Casaglia on 15 September. The BR 6th Armoured Division's advance along the Montone River valley towards Forlì was slowed by the terrain more than by the withdrawing 715.Infanterie-Division, its losses being mostly due to exposure. Unsurprisingly, even though on 18 September IND 8th Division seized the Casaglia Pass, the corps' advance continued to be slowed by the terrain and weather; the heavy rains in particular impeded its progress. With LI.Gebirgs-

Korps enforcing a methodical withdrawal, BR 1st Division's advance was halted on 25/26 September right outside Palazzuolo, to be resumed only after the German withdrawal.

Events soon overcame General Kirkman's decision to reserve the Borgo San Lorenzo–Marradi road only for BR 1st Division and IND 8th Division to advance towards Faenza along the Lamone River valley. As the latter was halted again on the 25th by German resistance, the advance was resumed four days later after the German withdrawal, just as US 88th Division's new situation required BR 1st Division to swing north in order to make contact. On 2 October, BR 78th Division joined the line, taking over from US 88th Division in the drive towards Imola along the Santerno valley, while BR 1st Division was diverted to advance along the Senio valley to Castel Bolognese. The BR XIII Corps soon faced stiffening German resistance as it advanced on an almost 40km-wide front without the support of corps troops.

A group of German soldiers in positions on the Apennine front, monitoring the approach of the enemy. (ullstein bild via Getty Images)

The BR 78th Division's advance was halted between 13 and 16 October by German resistance, just as BR 1st Division's advance was halted after a six-day battle. Only on the 16th was the division able to resume its advance, while IND 8th Division, after overcoming the German defences on the 7th, was itself soon halted. The same happened to BR 6th Armoured Division, whose lack of infantry prevented any further advance. By mid-October, as it became clear that XIII Corps' advance had stalled, General Kirkman decided to redeploy BR 6th Armoured Division between the BR 78th and 1st divisions in the Santerno valley, IND 8th Division being given the task of maintaining contact with the enemy on Route 67 towards Faenza. The British thrust towards Imola came to a halt as well. After seizing Monte La Pieve (which had been abandoned by the Germans) on 18/19 October, BR 78th Division continued its attacks on the nearby vantage points (Monte Spadaro, Monte Acqua Salata) on 19/20 October, but without success. The attack was renewed on the 23rd, leading to the seizure of Monte Spadaro, thanks to a further German withdrawal caused by pressure from BR 1st Infantry and 6th Armoured divisions, which had by then joined BR 1st Guards Brigade. In the meantime, IND 8th Division's advance had also halted because of stiffening German resistance.

On 22 October, BR 78th Division was diverted to support US II Corps' advance with an attack towards Imola, but worsening weather changed the situation by the following day. By 26 October, BR XIII Corps put a halt to its advance.

Clark's decision to abandon the thrust towards Imola was a pivotal one. There were good reasons not to carry on, such as US 88th Division's losses and stiffening German resistance, but Clark failed to realize that the Germans were facing a serious crisis. By mid-September, Kesselring's staff were already considering Operation *Herbstnebel*, Kesselring himself reacting the next day with sharp measures to prevent desertion and collapse among his troops. On

A 155mm gun of the BR 75th Highland Heavy Regiment, RA firing on German positions on 13 September 1944. Artillery provided constant support to the Allied armies throughout the entire Gothic Line campaign. (© Imperial War Museum, NA 18632)

the 17th, von Vietinghoff, himself taking *Herbstnebel* into account, asked for the release of 44.Infanterie-Division and suggested shortening the front. Three days later, Kesselring passed the suggestion on to the OKH, achieving Hitler's authorization the next day. However, Hitler only authorized local withdrawals, and he firmly opposed *Herbstnebel*. On 5 October, he refused to sanction a major withdrawal to the Alps.

All Kesselring managed to obtain of the 23,800 replacements he requested was the promise of 20,000. It must be recognized that while the German soldiers' endurance was severely tested in the weeks that followed, their morale held. On 20 September, Kesselring's chief of staff, General Röttiger, moved 44.Infanterie-Division (with one regiment already committed to defending the boundary between AOK 14 and 10) into the reserve, ready to face the advance of US 88th Division. Two days later, Kesselring authorized the withdrawal of LI.Gebirgs-Korps and I.Fallschirm-Korps to the Green Line II at Castel del Rio and the Radicosa Pass. In the meantime, 16.SS-Panzergrenadier-Division was to relieve 334.Infanterie-Division, itself to be deployed between 362. and 44.Infanterie-Division, while 94.Infanterie-Division was to be moved from the north to replace 71.Infanterie-Division as the weak 98.Infanterie-Division was brought back to LI.Gebirgs-Korps' front line.

On 25 September, the Allied Forces headquarters spotted the German withdrawal, and two days later Kesselring asked the OKH for authorization to enforce *Herbstnebel*, should they be unable to halt the enemy offensive. Hitler's refusal came that same day, with British intelligence aware of his response. On 28 September, Kesselring had a meeting with von Vietinghoff and Lemelsen, with whom he agreed to a progressive withdrawal, making the enemy pay for every inch of ground. The enemy thrust towards Imola was of the greatest concern, LI.Gebirgs-Korps having only 715 men and

44.Infanterie-Division facing the US 88th Division, so the decision was made to send reinforcements (comprising 334.Infanterie-Division) to join 98.Infanterie-Division. These were the last available units, all others (like 90.Panzergrenadier-Division, withdrawn from LXXVI.Panzer-Korps' front on 7 October) had to be made available by taking them from other sectors of the front.

Clark's decision brought much-needed relief, and by 4 October General Lemelsen had already noted that the enemy had switched from Imola to Bologna. The crisis was not over yet, but it seemed manageable. The major concern then was a possible landing in Istria, as German air reconnaissance had spotted ships in Ancona harbour. The decision to withdraw to the Erika Line on the Savio River coincided with intelligence reports revealing BR Eighth Army's manpower crisis. This, and Hitler's authorization to Kesselring to shorten the defensive line, enabled the redeployment of 29.Panzergrenadier-Division to face the US II Corps' advance towards Bologna. In early October, a new defensive line was created along the Idice and Reno rivers: the Gengis Khan Line.

At this point, the Germans faced a crisis of command. Kesselring, who had made his dissatisfaction with I.Fallschirm-Korps' commander General Schlemm clear, decided to shift the inter-army boundary and was relieved to know that Schlemm would be soon replaced by General Heidrich. So, the entire front between the Adriatic coast and Bologna would be put under AOK 10's command, which was to absorb XIV.Panzer-Korps (the command of which was switched with that of LI.Gebirgs-Korps) and I.Fallschirm-Korps. AOK 14 was to face only US IV Corps, and was formally subordinated to Armee-Gruppe Liguria (the army under Italian Field Marshal Rodolfo Graziani's command). These changes were announced on 23 October, becoming effective four days later. That same afternoon, Kesselring's car collided with a towed gun, putting the field marshal in hospital.

Von Vietinghoff replaced Kesselring, before himself being replaced by Lemelsen. On 24 October, General Heinz Ziegler took over AOK 14, but was wounded a month later in a partisan ambush. He was temporarily replaced by General Herr, until General Kurt von Tippelskirch took over on 12 December 1944. These changes did not prevent LXXVI.Panzer-Korps from being authorized to withdraw to the Ronco. Von Vietinghoff thought this was only a step on the journey, as on 24 October he asked Hitler for the authorization to carry out a fighting withdrawal to the Gengis Khan Line. Hitler refused, making US Fifth Army's drive towards Bologna the last, decisive act of the Gothic Line campaign.

US FIFTH ARMY'S DRIVE ON BOLOGNA

By 25 September, US II Corps' front line stood at the Radicosa Pass, which was seized by US 91st Division on the 28th/29th practically without a fight, since the division outflanked the German defences. Forced to pull back, the Germans deployed at Monghidoro, the first of a series of deep defensive lines running to the north at Loiano, then at Livergnano and at Pianoro. With the front now less than 40km by road away from Bologna, and with BR Eighth Army's offensive having reached the Romagna plain, the aim of reaching the Po River seemed within reach.

US Fifth Army and US IV Corps operations

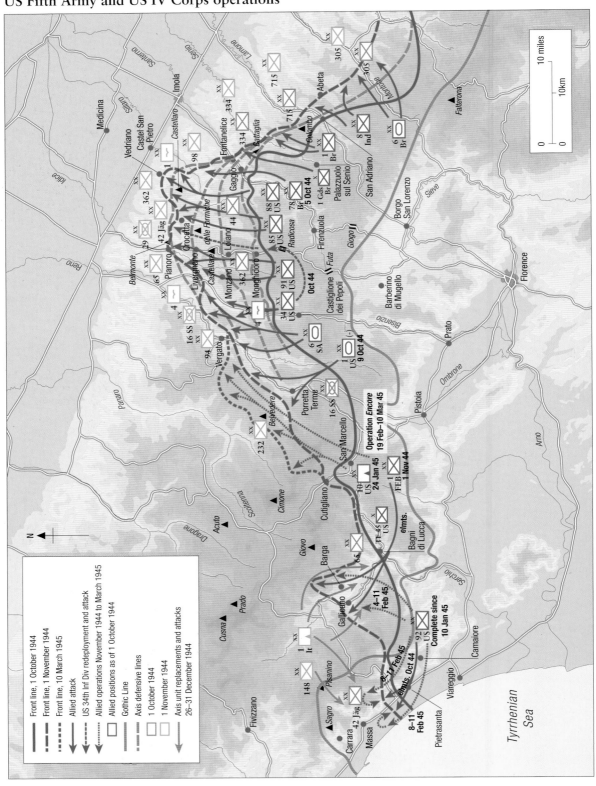

Front line, 1 October 1944

Front line, 1 November 1944

Front line, 10 March 1945

Allied attack

US 34th Inf Div redeployment and attack

Allied operations November 1944 to March 1945

Allied positions as of 1 October 1944

Gothic Line

Axis defensive lines

1 October 1944

1 November 1944

Axis unit replacements and attacks
26–31 December 1944

US II Corps' commander General Keyes decided to attack on a broad front with all four divisions under his command. Given the lack of reserves (US 1st Armored Division being of little value in mountainous terrain), each division was to hold one regiment in reserve, rotating it with the attacking ones every five days. The idea was for US 91st Division to attack on a 6km front astride Route 65 to Bologna with US 85th Division to its right, which was to attack along the Sillaro River valley on a 10km front. To the west, US 34th Division was to protect the corps' left flank, while to the east US 88th Division,

'Rover Joe' in action in October 1944. Rover Joe was the name given to the ground-to-air liaison units (usually made up of ex-pilots) that coordinated air attacks on Axis positions. (NARA)

about to be relieved by BR 78th Division, was to move between the Sillaro and Santerno river valleys before swinging north to the former. The SA 6th Armoured Division, with attached elements from US 1st Armored Division, was put under direct US Fifth Army command to ensure the link-up with US IV Corps.

General Clark's orders, issued on 5 October, set the aim of breaking into the Po valley in an area between the west of Bologna and Faenza in order to establish a bridgehead on the Po north of Bologna. This meant that if the German units facing BR Eighth Army were trapped south of the Lake Comacchio area, the army was to drive towards Ferrara to close the pocket. Alternatively, if the Germans withdrew, both US Fifth and BR Eighth armies were to converge on Bologna with the former in the lead. In the meantime, US IV Corps was to advance to Genoa and Parma in order to secure the necessary supply roads.

US Fifth Army's offensive was launched at 0600hrs on 1 October, with US II Corps attacking on a 16km front facing the German I.Fallschirm-Korps comprising the worn-out 4.Fallschirmjäger-Division, 362.Infanterie-Division and 44.Infanterie-Division, the area having been neglected in favour of Monte Battaglia and the threat posed there by US 88th Division. The seven American regiments in the lead were blessed both by a sunny day and by a German withdrawal, leading to minor rearguard engagements. On 2 October, the weather changed, but German tactics didn't, the latter based on pulling back whenever a position was outflanked or overrun. The Monghidoro line was held until the 4th, marking the end of US II Corps' rapid advance and the start of the new phase of the offensive now facing the Loiano line.

US 91st Division, moving from a line 1.5km south of Monghidoro with five battalions from 363rd and 362nd RCTs, initially made slight gains, despite enjoying heavy artillery support. Monghidoro was seized on 2 October and, as a night attack led to the breaching of the German defences, on the 3rd, thanks to the German withdrawal, the division advanced to 1.5km south of Loiano. Its slow progress was due to the stubborn defence put up by 4.Fallschirmjäger-Division. On the 4th, an attack on Loiano stalled when an American tank was destroyed on the road by an anti-tank gun, blocking it. The US 85th Division, advancing along the divide between the Idice and the Sillaro rivers, was led by the 339th and 337th RCTs. The first

COMPANY K, US 361ST RCT AT LIVERGNANO, 10 OCTOBER 1944 (PP. 66–67)

Having been tasked with taking the town of Livergnano, where Route 65 (**1**) cuts a passage through the 5km-long escarpment (**2**), I./361st RCT of US 91st Division faced a German counter-attack that was successfully repulsed, the enemy being driven back into the town. At this point, Captain Chatlain Sigman, Company K's commander, led the 3rd Platoon forward and, using the misty conditions for concealment, stormed into Livergnano only to be forced by German machine-gun fire to take cover in a large house in the centre of the town (**3**), while ten other men took shelter in a nearby pigsty. After dark, Captain Sigman gathered the rest of Company K at Livergnano and set up a defensive strongpoint in the large building with about 80 men.

From dawn the following day, the Germans, having spotted the location of Company K, began shelling the house with heavy mortar fire. A first German attack took place shortly after dawn, but it was repulsed. The other companies of the US 1st Battalion, attempting to reach Livergnano to help Company K, were held back by German fire from the escarpment, and problems with communications added further complications. In late morning, the Germans attacked again, this time with the support of a self-propelled gun (**4**), and eventually they managed to reach and take the building, capturing the remnants of Company K. Only the ten men who were sheltering in the pigsty were able to make their way back to 1st Battalion under cover of darkness.

encountered strong German resistance on the 2nd approaching the Idice, and was relieved by 338th RCT on 4/5 October. The 337th RCT was able to break through the German defences thanks to armoured support, only to face German counter-attacks. On 3 October, a new attack led to heavy casualties, but the German defensive line was broken through the next day.

Facing 98.Infanterie-Division deployed on both sides of the Idice, US 85th Division consolidated its gains, while on the 5th, US 91st Division attacked Loiano with three regiments, facing the fresh 65.Infanterie-Division. A hard fight ensued, the Germans being eventually compelled to pull back and redeploy between Loiano and the Livergnano escarpment. On the 7th, US 91st Division attacked the dominating peak of Monte Castellare, which was seized after a two-day fight. This allowed 361st RCT to advance swiftly to the north-east and penetrate deep into enemy lines, until it was halted on 9 October by a German counter-attack from Livergnano.

A US tank battalion prepares to support the attack on Monghidoro, 1 October 1944. The role played by tanks in the US Fifth Army's drive on Bologna was limited because of the unsuitable terrain. (US Army)

The Livergnano position was a formidable one, a 5km-long rock escarpment in some places up to 450m high, dominated, east of Livergnano, by Monte delle Formiche (about halfway between Livergnano and the Idice), which remained unbroken save for only in a few places, such as at the town of Livergnano itself. The experience of US I./361st RCT showed how hard breaking through the line would be. Its Company K entered Livergnano on 9 October only to be trapped and destroyed by German counter-attacks. On that day, as US 338th RCT of US 85th Division moved along the Idice to Monte delle Formiche, other units from US 361st RCT were able to scale the escarpment, only to find themselves isolated and subjected to enemy fire.

Defended by a mixture of German units (elements from Grenadier-Regiment 267 from 94.Infanterie-Division, Grenadier-Regiment 956 from 362.Infanterie-Division and Grenadier-Regiment 147 from 65.Infanterie-Division), Monte delle Formiche was attacked by US 338th RCT at 0800hrs on 10 October. One US company managed to storm the peak by mid-afternoon, despite being subjected to heavy German artillery fire. German counter-attacks materialized almost immediately, and all were repulsed as the rest of US 338th RCT swung west to join US 91st Division's attack on the Livergnano escarpment. This marked the end of US 85th Division's advance; facing strong defences on the northern slopes of Monte delle Formiche, US 338th RCT was only able to advance less than 1.5km during the next three days, until the Germans withdrew to their new defensive line. The rest of US 85th Division continued to advance along the Idice River valley until 13 October, when, after clearing the Monterenzio hill feature, US 337th RCT was relieved by US 339th RCT.

A view of Livergnano from the south, showing the final stretch of Route 65 and the approach to the town. First damaged by shelling during the fighting, Livergnano was razed to the ground by German shelling in the attempt to block the highway. (US Army)

The Livergnano escarpment area was defended by a mixture of units including II./Fallschirmjäger-Regiment 10 and II./Grenadier-Regiment 145 to the west, I./Grenadier-Regiment 146 at Livergnano, and II./Grenadier-Regiment 146 and the divisional reconnaissance echelon to the east. After Company K's destruction, it was outflanked to the west by US 361st RCT and to the east by US 363rd RCT. On 10 October, the latter, at first assisting the attack on Monte delle Formiche, was diverted against Livergnano, given the stiff German resistance. On the 11th, it succeeded in launching a night attack against the eastern slope of the escarpment, just as US I./361st RCT succeeded in outflanking the village from the west and placing a platoon atop the escarpment on the 12th. Even though this was driven back by a German counter-attack, by the end of the day eight American infantry companies followed to the top of the escarpment, eventually outflanking Livergnano. In the end, the combined effect of infantry attacks, artillery fire and air bombardment cracked the German defences on 13 October and, as the Americans reached the dominating positions above Livergnano the next day, eventually the Germans withdrew.

To the east, US 88th Division was initially able to commit only its 349th RCT and one battalion of the 351st RCT before being relieved by 4 October; even then the units needed rest, while those committed faced German resistance until the 3rd. After the German withdrawal, US 88th Division reached Monte del Falchetto by 6–7 October, seizing the hill the following day as the Germans withdrew again. By 9 October, the division had reached the town of Gesso, where 754.Grenadier-Regiment stabilized the defence and repulsed the American attacks. Only on 13–14 October was the division able to resume its advance after crossing the Sillaro, exploiting a gap in the German defences, which enabled US 350th RCT to advance north, keeping abreast of the other units until its progress was halted at the Gesso ridge.

Advancing along a 6km front to the west, US 34th Division pressed forward after seizing Monte del Falchetto on 3 October, which led to the withdrawal of 16.SS-Panzergrenadier-Division's units. Rather than on account of the German defences, the divisional advance was slowed down by the need to secure the corps' flank and mop up German pockets of resistance, a task undertaken by US 165th RCT until it was relieved on 9–10 October by a screening force from US 91st Cavalry Reconnaissance Squadron. By the 7th, the division was advancing towards Monterumici (south of Monzano), its units inching forward to the new German line of defence, which was reached two days later.

At this point, an assessment could be made of the achievements of US II Corps. After the first four days, in spite of the slow pace of advance (1.5km per day) and relatively high losses (between 1 and 15 October the four divisions had lost 5,699 men), it was still reckoned that access to the Po valley could be achieved before the rain turned to snow. The German defences had been pierced at Livergnano and Monte delle Formiche, but the strain on the Allied infantry was beginning to show its effects. On 10–11 October, the US 34th Division's attack against Monterumici failed, its axis of advance being handed to SA 6th Armoured Division just as it was being given fresh orders.

On the 10th, General Keyes decided to focus on US 91st Division's advance, to be supported by US 34th Division, which was to be replaced by CCA of US 1st Armored Division. On 13–14 October, US 34th Division redeployed at Monte delle Formiche, with the aim of advancing along the Idice River valley to cut the main road east of Bologna. To the left, US 91st Division was to continue along Route 65, the two units being supported by US 85th Division advancing along the Sillaro.

The problem for the Allies was that Kesselring had realized that the enemy's main effort was in the US Fifth Army area, and reacted accordingly. He sent reinforcements taken from the BR Eighth Army area (such as 29.Panzergrenadier-Division, followed at the end of November by 1.Fallschirmjäger-Division and elements from 90.Panzergrenadier-Division) redeployed east of Bologna to replenish those lost. Adding these unexpected difficulties to the American advance, from 10 November US Fifth Army had started to experience artillery ammunition shortages as well, and it was soon clear that no matter how close Bologna was, the road ahead was still a long one.

Two US infantrymen watch the artillery shelling of the town of Livergnano, on 18 October 1944. (PhotoQuest/Getty Images)

At 0500hrs on 16 October, two regiments from US 34th Division jumped off from Monte delle Formiche, advancing towards Monte Belmonte. German resistance slowed their progress, and only the following day did the lead elements of US 133rd RCT near the southern slopes of Monte Belmonte, at which point a counter-attack by elements from 29.Panzergrenadier-Division drove them back, wiping out a company. A new attempt the next day saw US 133rd RCT halted at first by the unfamiliar terrain, and then driven back by another German counter-attack supported by tanks. Since the neighbouring US 168th RCT was also making slow progress, General Charles Bolté ordered them to regroup, which effectively halted the advance. Meanwhile, US 91st Division, which hampered by fire from Monte Belmonte and the terrain only advanced 1.5km north of Livergnano in four days, was ordered on the 19th to adopt an 'aggressive defence'.

The US 34th Division's failure led to another change of plan. On 19 October, Clark ordered that US 88th Division

An ordnance outfit attached to the US 91st Division provides hot meals for the soldiers resting after the fight for Bologna, December 1944. (PhotoQuest/Getty Images)

should take the lead by attacking Monte Grande, supported by US 337th RCT of US 85th Division, itself supporting the attack to the west. The attack, which began at 0700hrs on the 19th with heavy artillery and air support, got off to a promising start as US 88th Division's 349th RCT neared Monte Grande that same day, successfully repulsing a German counter-attack. By midday the following day, US 349th RCT had seized Monte Grande, as the rest of US 88th Division progressed to the east while US 85th Division advanced to the west, with the rest of US II Corps remaining static. This success led Clark to visit the front, clearly hoping that he would enjoy victory soon.

On 22 October, US 85th Division attacked Monte Castellaro while US 88th Division targeted the town of Vedriano, the latter's 351st RCT repulsing a counter-attack by elements from 90.Panzergrenadier-Division the next day. Vedriano was taken on the 24th, but German strongpoints halted any further advances and a German counter-attack saw the place being retaken that same day. On 25 October, US 351st RCT, largely composed of green replacements, made another attempt against Vedriano. Not only did the attack disintegrate, but a German counter-attack saw two American companies surrounded and another one practically destroyed during a further counter-attack on the 26th. This, and the heavy rain that flooded the entire area, led General Keyes to halt the offensive about 16km short of Bologna.

In October alone, US Fifth Army suffered 13,140 casualties, its four divisions having lost a total of 15,716 casualties since 10 September (5,026 within US 88th Division alone). German losses in October are estimated at some 17,000. Given the lack of replacements, General Clark was not wrong in concluding that the offensive failed because of a lack of strength.

US M10 tank destroyers fire in support of the infantry south of Bologna, 8 December 1944. The terrain and the lack of enemy armour saw these units employed in this type of support. (Corbis via Getty Images)

BR EIGHTH ARMY'S FINAL PUSH

At the end of October 1944, BR Eighth Army faced the strain of prolonged battle. It had a shortage of infantry, whose morale was affected by issues such as the rationing of provisions and ammunition (by 1 November, the average rounds per day issued to each gun had dropped from 36.5 to 31.12). Also, on 2 November, BR 1st Division was withdrawn. By now, the weather had started to become more wintry.

Unsurprisingly, the plan devised during the 29 October conference by British General Charles Keightley focused on close objectives. The BR Eighth Army was to reach positions that could enable it to attack Ravenna from the west, starting from the Via Emilia, a direct attack along the coastline being ruled out due to the marshy terrain. Keightley's plan envisaged that BR V Corps would cross the Ronco, establish bridgeheads on the Montone along the Via Emilia and from there exploit the advance by seizing Faenza. The attack was to be spearheaded by BR 4th and IND 10th divisions north of Cesena, at the Meldola bridgehead, while BR 46th Division was to attack along the Via Emilia. To the west, BR Eighth Army's drive was supported by POL II Corps, which was to take over from BR 6th Armoured at Rocca San Casciano and advance north to threaten Forlì.

As the ground dried at the Meldola bridgehead, on 30 October IND 10th Division attacked, followed the next day by BR 4th Division, which crossed the Ronco without problems. German resistance was rather weak, with the exception of the airport south of Forlì where the BR 4th Division faced a tough fight. By 1–2 November, IND 10th Division had reached Grisignano. Also on 1 November, delayed by transport issues, POL 3rd Division attacked, advancing northwards, south-east of Modigliana, while POL 5th Division advanced north-west approaching the Montone River, but was soon halted by German resistance. The Poles and IND 10th Division were soon to be relieved by BR 46th Division. On 2 November, pouring rain halted BR V Corps' operations, enabling BR 46th Division to relieve IND 10th Division the following day. Facing stiffening German resistance, Keightley decided

A group of Fallschirmjäger running to take cover in a city in Romagna, October 1944. The vehicle in the background is the Italian copy of the Daimler Dingo scout car. (Keystone/ Getty Images)

BR Eighth Army's push to Faenza and the river battles, November 1944–January 1945

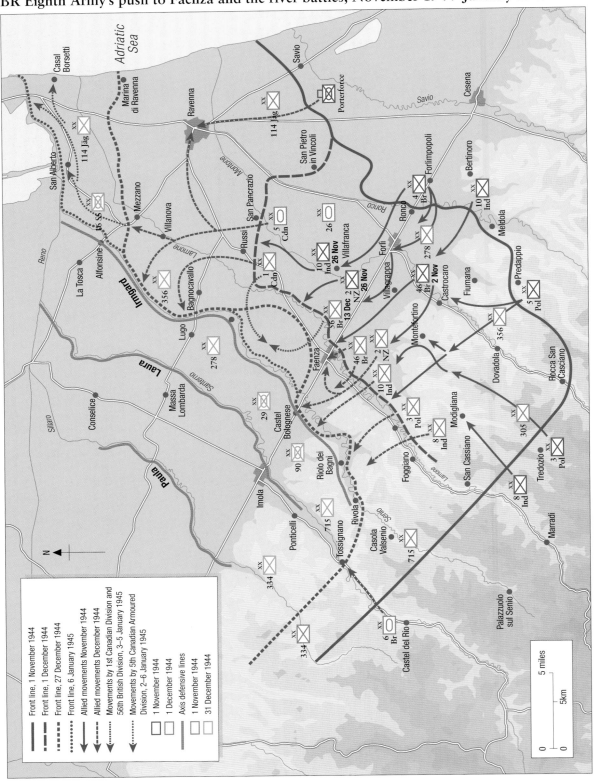

on a two-pronged attack, with BR 4th Division moving against Forlì and, on a parallel route, BR 46th Division advancing south-west with the aim of reaching the Montone River, seizing a bridge intact and exploiting towards Faenza. If that proved impossible, the two divisions were to reach the Montone and secure a bridgehead north of Forlì.

The BR 4th Division attacked on 7 November, fighting its way into Forlì over the following two days. In order to avoid delays, its 12th Brigade attacked north of the city towards the Montone using a narrow corridor between two ditches. The attack, launched on 10 November, faced resistance from a battalion from 278.Infanterie-Division and the Maschinengehwer-Bataillon 'Feldmarschall Kesselring' (an elite machine-gun battalion), which led to house-to-house fighting in which the Germans used armour to defend each single building until driven out by artillery and air support.

A BR Eighth Army column enters the town of Forlì in November 1944. (Wartimepd/Alamy)

The German defences were broken through on the 11th and, after a counter-attack by 278.Infanterie-Division failed, the way ahead lay open for BR 4th Division. Held up by flooding, BR 46th Division was only able to cross the Montone south of Forlì on 11/12 November, just as the first elements of 26.Panzer-Division arrived in the area. Having made contact with POL 3rd Division on the 9th, the division was then given the task of enlarging the bridgehead and advancing northwards to reach Faenza. Meanwhile, BR 4th Division was to advance north of the Via Emilia, crossing the Montone and exploiting the bridgehead to secure a crossing of the Lamone River north-east of Faenza. A composite brigade from BR 56th Division was to take over the advance along the Via Emilia to distract the German defenders.

The initial success enjoyed by BR V Corps was due to the collapse of one regiment from 356.Infanterie-Division, which led von Vietinghoff to ask for permission to withdraw using delaying tactics. Even though Hitler would refuse permission on 17 November, insisting that LXXVI.Panzer-Korps must stand its ground and create reserves, already on the 10th General Herr had authorized the withdrawal of both 356. and 278.Infanterie-Division to Forlì, after von Vietinghoff had reported two days before to the OKH that the enemy had broken through and was advancing into Forlì, forcing its abandonment. As a result, 278.Infanterie-Division was ordered to withdraw north and north-west of Forlì, in spite of its early effective defence, while Herr ordered 26.Panzer-Division to swap positions with 356.Infanterie-Division. At this point, German intelligence had revealed that concerns over a renewed American offensive towards Bologna were unfounded, which enabled Hitler to order that Forlì be held at least until the 13th, as the battle for the city turned into the battle for the Montone River.

The German predicament was made worse by the Polish advance on either side of the Montone River valley, eased by the crisis facing 305.Infanterie-

A Polish soldier bandages a comrade's hand as the fighting continues in Emilia-Romagna, 25 November 1944. (Mondadori via Getty Images)

Division. By 11 November, POL 5th Division had cleared the eastern side of the valley that linked with BR 46th Division, but Polish progress was being hampered by difficulties with supplies, following the collapse of a Bailey bridge, which also halted the divisional artillery of POL 3rd Division. The IND 8th Division, advancing with its three brigades on a wide front in the Senio River valley towards Castel Bolognese to tie down German forces, did not provide much support, since it faced no serious German opposition until reaching Modigliana on the 11th. On 12/13 November, the worn-out POL 5th Division, due to be relieved, broke through on the Montone to reach Monte Cerreto, west of Castrocaro. Meanwhile, to the west, POL 3rd Division continued its advance towards Montefortino, being partly relieved on the 14th by the composite 18th Brigade, which entered Modigliana along with elements from IND 8th Division.

On 12 November, the BR 4th Division's advance still faced stubborn resistance, until the next day when 278. Infanterie-Division fell back across the Montone. The BR 4th Division reached the latter on the 14th – to the north of Faenza – but found no suitable place to cross. While a brigade from BR 56th Division advanced along the Via Emilia, a battalion from BR 46th Division seized Monte Poggiolo west of Forlì, without difficulties. Monte Poggiolo had been defended by elements from 20.Luftwaffe-Feld-Division, which had been incorporated into 26.Panzer-Division; on the 12th, the latter was authorized to pull back to the Montone. The withdrawal was completed in two days, but by the 16th, BR V Corps' advance had been checked already.

Allied troops cross the Lamone River, passing a destroyed tracked vehicle. (Keystone-France/Gamma-Rapho via Getty Images)

At the same time, POL II Corps progressed by seizing mounts Cerreto and Casale, but as General Władysław Anders saw necessary to secure communications before proceeding, General McCreery asked him to seize Montefortino in order to secure BR 46th Division's flank. Allowed the use of BR V Corps' routes, Anders sent forward his only reserve, POL 2nd Carpathian Brigade, which was held up by rain and was eventually replaced by POL 5th Division. The latter, with BR 46th Division's help, on 17 November seized Montefortino, where it faced a prompt and determined counter-attack executed by 26.Panzer-Division.

On 19 November, Alexander's chief of staff General Sir John Harding evaluated the situation in Italy. With BR Eighth Army's operations stalling and US Fifth Army's inactivity, the Germans had been able to place 90.Panzergrenadier-Division and 362.Infanterie-Division in reserve, while I.Fallschirm-Korps units were rotated and replenished. Facing the fact that there would be no German withdrawal to the Po and that US Fifth Army's rest and reorganization would not be completed before early December, it was assessed that BR Eighth Army (which had completed its own reorganization) could reach the Santerno River, securing bridgeheads by December. Only then would it be possible to decide whether to launch a major offensive in December or not.

New Zealand soldiers examine a 75mm shell found in a German tank, November 1944. (Mondadori via Getty Images)

On 18 November, General McCreery ordered the clearance of the Montone bridgehead in order to provide starting positions for CDN I Corps, while BR V Corps was to cross the Lamone and seize Faenza. The task of clearing the area to the east towards Russi was given to IND 10th Division, while the NZ 2nd and BR 56th divisions were due to replace the BR 4th and 46th divisions. The latter had broken through the German defences on the Via Emilia, clearing Castiglione (west of Villagrappa) by the 20th, securing the starting positions for their attack along the road.

At 0200hrs on the 21st, BR 4th Division attacked, crossing a ditch running south from the Montone, and running into minefields while facing strong German defences, so a halt to the operation was brought about. The attack was repeated during the night of 22/23 November by both BR 4th and 46th divisions, which was successful beyond the ditches forming the German line of defence, just as POL II Corps seized Monte Ricci to the south of Faenza. Faced with this attack, von Vietinghoff had no choice, since concern over an American offensive towards Bologna did not warrant committing any reserves. On the 23rd, he authorized 26.Panzer-Division to withdraw across the Marzeno stream, running parallel to the Lamone south of Faenza, which it did that same day along with the 305. and 278.Infanterie divisions. Even though both 356.Infanterie-Division and 114.Jäger-Division still held their positions, this was the beginning of a withdrawal to the Lamone, which was von Vietinghoff's only way to shorten the front and create reserves.

New Zealand soldiers advancing among the ruins of the town of Faenza, 20 December 1944. (Mondadori via Getty Images)

On 24 November, 26.Panzer-Division could not oppose BR 46th Division's attack, which, by 1100hrs, had reached the outskirts of Faenza, only to find the main bridge destroyed. As the division secured the ground between the Montone and the Lamone, during the night of 25/26 November 26.Panzer-Division fell back behind the Lamone along with 305.Infanterie-Division. The BR 46th Division then approached the river, but preparations for the crossing were slowed by rain.

By the 28th, POL 5th Division had also reached the Lamone to the south. The advance of BR 4th Division also proceeded swiftly until slowed by the rearguards of 278.Infanterie-Division 5km east of the Lamone, where the division was replaced by NZ 2nd Division. After crossing the Montone on the 25th, IND 10th Division faced stiff resistance and was halted before Russi, with 278.Infanterie-Division still holding the Casa Bettini hamlet to the south. This was seized on 30 November, with the aid of heavy artillery support and the New Zealanders. The division reached the German military bridge on the Lamone, but found it destroyed.

With rain having begun to fall on 23 November, on the 26th General Keightley ordered the crossing of the Lamone on a broad front with NZ 2nd Division (which had relieved BR 4th Division on the 26th) and BR 56th Division (which relieved BR 46th Division on the 30th). In the meantime, CDN I Corps also prepared to take command of Porterforce, while on 1 December CDN 1st Division relieved IND 10th Division, which was to advance west of Russi.

Keightley's orders for BR Eighth Army's last offensive in 1944 gave CDN I Corps the task of advancing towards Russi and cutting the Via Adriatica north-west of Ravenna, before crossing the Santerno near Massa Lombarda. The BR V Corps was to advance along the Via Emilia establishing bridgeheads on the Lamone, the Senio and the Santerno, while POL II Corps was to protect its left flank by threatening Imola with a parallel advance between the Senio and the Santerno. The BR XIII Corps would also advance with IND 8th Division and BR 6th Armoured astride the Senio and Santerno valleys.

Eventually, the terrain forced some changes to the BR V Corps plan. The BR 46th Division, before being relieved, was to cross south of Faenza and swing north to cut the road, while the NZ 2nd Division and IND 10th Division staged feint attacks. In case of failure, the two divisions would then switch to BR 46th Division's sector and cross the river. General Charles Foulkes, CDN I Corps' new commander, gave CDN 1st Division the task of advancing to Russi and Massa, while the CDN 5th Armoured Division was to swing north to the Via Adriatica and Ravenna.

Nepalese Gurkha soldiers advancing north of Faenza in December 1944. (Mondadori via Getty Images)

During the night of 2/3 December, CDN I Corps opened the offensive. The CDN 1st Division seized Russi on the 3rd, then advanced north-west to the Lamone. Although the river was reached, no bridgehead could be established. The division also suffered heavy losses. The CDN 5th Division, facing the withdrawal of both 114.Jäger-Division and 305.Infanterie-Division (whose boundaries had been hit), pressed forwards and turned towards Ravenna, which was reached on 4 December, accompanied by Porterforce and some Italian partisans who had also joined in the fighting. By 6 December, CDN 5th Armoured Division had also reached the banks of the Lamone to the north.

As the NZ 2nd and IND 10th divisions staged their feint attacks, during the night of 3/4 December, and faced the reaction of 26.Panzer-Division and 278.Infanterie-Division, BR 46th Division crossed the Lamone. It encountered little resistance from 305.Infanterie-Division, but its advance was slowed by rain that caused the Lamone to flood on 6/7 December. Nevertheless, the entire division was across the river by the 7th, just as POL

A mortar company of the US 92nd Division rapidly fires on German machine-gun nests in order to liquidate them, near Massa in November 1944. (NARA)

Shermans from the Canadian 5th Armoured Division provide indirect support during the advance towards Ravenna, 4 December 1944. (Universal Images Group via Getty Images)

3rd Division also crossed the river and seized Monte San Rinaldo, to the south-west of Faenza. That same day, Keightley decided to regroup, with the NZ 2nd and IND 10th divisions taking over from BR 46th Division.

On 4 December, von Vietinghoff eventually decided to commit 90.Panzergrenadier-Division, with the aim of fighting a staged withdrawal to the Gengis Khan Line. On the 7th, Hitler refused to give his authorization for a withdrawal. The LXXVI.Panzer-Korps had to stand and fight, and both 98.Infanterie-Division and 29.Panzergrenadier-Division were to follow suit. On 9 December, Panzergrenadier-Regiment 200 of 90.Panzergrenadier-Division launched a counter-attack west of Faenza against BR 46th Division's 138th Brigade. The brigade suffered heavy losses, but the Germans failed to

Allied traffic on the road to Ravenna, 7 December 1944. The sign is revealing of the situation at the end of the Gothic Line campaign: stress and exhaustion led to behaviour that endangered civilians and their property. (Photo by Sergeant Bowman/Imperial War Museums via Getty Images)

New Zealand infantry cross the Lamone River via ruins of the destroyed bridge, Faenza, 20 December 1944. (Mondadori via Getty Images)

eradicate the bridgehead. On 10 December, both the NZ 2nd and IND 10th divisions crossed the Lamone, leapfrogging BR 46th Division.

On the night of 10/11 December, the CDN 1st and 5th Armoured divisions crossed the Lamone in the area between Bagnacavallo and Alfonsine, taking the Germans by surprise. The German reserves (98.Infanterie-Division and 90.Panzergrenadier-Division) were committed, and a counter-attack was launched on the 12th. However, it failed to dislodge the Canadians, leading the Germans to deploy along the parallel Naviglio Canal, which the Canadians tried to cross that same day. The CDN 1st Division successfully established a bridgehead north of Bagnacavallo, which on the 13th CDN 5th Division used to cross the river after its failure to the north. Facing the entire 98.Infanterie-Division, both divisions stalled and the offensive was halted on 14/15 December. From 16 to 18 December, CDN 1st Division attempted to seize Bagnacavallo, without success. However, a new attack to reach the Senio was successful, but losses were heavy as the river was approached on the 21st.

Also on 14/15 December, NZ 2nd Division, with Indian support, attacked 26.Panzer-Division, which withdrew to the Senio, being eventually replaced by 29.Panzergrenadier-Division on the 17th. Four days later, 16.SS-Panzergrenadier-Division deployed north of Imola. By 16 December, 43rd Gurkha Brigade had cleared Faenza, while IND 10th Division had neared the Senio, establishing a bridgehead by the next day. On the 19th, NZ 2nd Division attacked and reached the river, just as Keightley ordered the division, along with BR 56th Division, to clear the area between the Lamone and the Senio and link up with CDN I Corps. On that same day the first snow fell. On 2 January 1945, during a conference with generals Clark, McCreery and Truscott, Field Marshal Alexander called a halt to the offensive. The Gothic Line campaign was nearing its end, but was not quite over yet.

FINAL OPERATIONS

Early in November 1944, both BRZ 1st FEB (from 1 November) and the African-American 'Buffalo' US 92nd Division (from the 8th) had been fully deployed at the front in US IV Corps' area. The Brazilians were on the left wing of US II Corps, and US 92nd Division was on the coast at the westernmost flank of US IV Corps, which on 4 November had the SA 6th Division under command again. With an 80km-wide front and many untested units, US IV Corps could only carry out training and limited operations.

On 6 October 1944, BRZ 1st FEB's 6th RCT attacked the positions held by the Italian Monte Rosa Division in the Serchio River valley, seizing the town of Barga. On that same day US TF 92 had its 370th RCT, along with US 2nd Armored Group, attacking along the coast towards Massa. Facing the still-intact Gothic Line defences and German counter-attacks, the operation achieved only modest results until it was called off on 23 October. Subsequently, US IV Corps' front remained inactive for 1½ months.

In November 1944, following Kesselring's reorganization of the command, the German 148.Infanterie-Division and 232.Infanterie-Division were deployed facing US IV Corps, along with the Italian Monte Rosa Division, reinforced with elements from the Italian 'San Marco' and the German 157.Gebirgsjäger-Division. Facing the green US 92nd Division, AOK 14 decided to carry out a limited offensive in the Serchio River valley. Commencing on 26 December 1944, Operation *Wintergewitter* (*Winter Storm*) was spearheaded by elements of 148.Infanterie-Division reinforced by Gebirgsjäger-Lehr-Bataillon 'Mittenwald' (a mountain-troop training unit), plus elements from the Monte Rosa Division. Taking US 92nd Division by surprise, the Germans (followed by the Italians) advanced some 25km into

A column of African-American US 92nd Division troops on the move with tank support, in late 1944. The division's attack along the Tyrrhenian coast ended in failure. (NARA)

US infantrymen on the march in the Monte Belvedere area. The last operation of the Gothic Line campaign was to secure the starting positions for the 1945 Allied spring offensive. (US Army)

US IV Corps' lines before withdrawing the next day. The entire operation – essentially a reconnaissance in force – caused great concern among the Allied commanders, who promptly dispatched IND 8th Division's 19th Brigade to restore the situation. It is claimed that this was a contributory factor to the last offensive being called off.

As the offensives were halted, both the BR Eighth and US Fifth armies carried out limited operations to consolidate their front lines. Between 3 and 5 January 1945, CDN 1st Division, along with BR 56th Division, cleared the Granarolo salient east of the Senio River, the former attacking from the north and the latter from the south. This neat operation, concluded with minimal losses, witnessed for the first time the employment of the 'Kangaroo' modified armoured personnel carrier.

This operation was matched on 2 January 1945 by CDN 5th Armoured Division's attack towards the Valli di Comacchio (the Comacchio Valleys, in reality a mix of marshy areas and lakes). Taking advantage of the frozen ground, the division attacked in the Mezzano area heading north for the Reno River, initially facing stiff German resistance. During this first phase, the Germans launched a series of small counter-attacks, which were easily

Soldiers of the 92nd Division pause for rest and warmth in the ruins of an Italian house. The 92nd's divisional symbol, a buffalo, can be seen on the left shoulder of the man on the right. (NARA)

'BUFFALO' INFANTRY ATTACK IN THE SERCHIO RIVER VALLEY, FEBRUARY 1945 (PP. 84–85)

On 4 February 1945, US 365th RCT and elements from US 366th RCT attacked the German positions on either side of the Serchio River from Gallicano to Barga. After relieving the 3rd Battalion during the night of 7/8 February, III./365th RCT was driven back from its newly taken positions at Monte della Stella by a counter-attack led by II./Grenadier-Regiment 286. On 10 February, the US II. and III./365th RCT, supported by the attached II./366th RCT, attacked the German positions to retake Monte della Stella, and this time encountered lighter opposition from the Italian light infantry of the 1a Divisione Bersaglieri 'Italia' (**1**). After taking 55 prisoners, the African-American soldiers from US 92nd Division entered the village of Lama, only to face a series of German counter-attacks that stalled the American advance, before it was finally brought to a close on 11 February.

For the first time, in the winter of 1944/45 US infantrymen were equipped with a suitable winter uniform, comprising the M1943 Field Jacket (**2**), worn here by the majority of soldiers, along with the newly issued M1943 Combat Service Boots (**3**). The M1919 .30-cal. machine-gun team leader (**4**) is an exception, as he wears the 1st-pattern mackinaw (or short coat) in characteristic olive drab. An officer, displaying a stripe on the back of his helmet (**5**), wears the 1941 Tanker Jacket, a common piece of clothing worn by US infantry officers at the time. The Italian Bersaglieri, partly kitted out with German equipment and clothing, display their characteristic black feathered cockerel on their helmets and a mixture of old grey-green uniforms and windproof jackets.

An M10 tank destroyer supporting the US 10th Mountain Division moves on a mountain road overlooking a Bailey bridge, built among the ruins of a town. (NARA)

repulsed by the Canadians, who then advanced towards the Reno. Conscious of the strategic importance of the area, on 4 January 1945 LXXVI.Panzer-Korps launched a major counter-attack with I./SS-Panzergrenadier-Regiment 36 plus the reconnaissance battalion from 16.SS-Panzergrenadier-Division, supported by the reconnaissance battalions from 26.Panzer and 114.Jäger divisions. Lacking artillery support, which the Canadians had in abundance, the attack, aimed at the Mezzano area, ended in failure as CDN 5th Division swept to the coast south of the Reno. The operation cost the Germans at least 300 killed and 600 prisoners taken for some 200 Canadian casualties.

On 28 December 1944, General Truscott had instructed General Willis Crittenberger to prepare an operation aimed at improving the US Fifth Army positions north of Viareggio, so that La Spezia harbour could be exploited. Operation *Fourth Term* was to be supported by a diversion in the Serchio River valley, which, on 4 February 1945, saw the US 92nd Division's 365th and 366th RCTs attacking the German positions near Barca. The attack was called off on the 7th following a German counter-attack. On 8 February 1945, US 92nd Division's 370th and 371st RCTs attacked once again along the coast, but were soon halted by minefields and a determined German counter-attack. This unsuccessful operation was called off on the 11th. The US 92nd Division had proved itself on the battlefield, but at the cost of 47 officers and 659 other ranks.

US IV CORPS ADVANCES ALONG THE RENO RIVER, 3–9 MARCH 1945

On 3 March 1945, the second phase of Operation *Encore* began; US 10th Mountain and BRZ 1st FEB divisions attacked along the Belvedere–Torraccia mountains west of the Reno River. The aim was to consolidate suitable positions for the spring offensive towards Bologna, with US 10th Mountain Division opening the way and BRZ 1st FEB consolidating the positions along its route. Once again, the collaboration between the two units was excellent, so much so that Kesselring was concerned that this could be the start of a major offensive, and committed his last available reserves. The conclusion of the operation brought to an end the Gothic Line campaign.

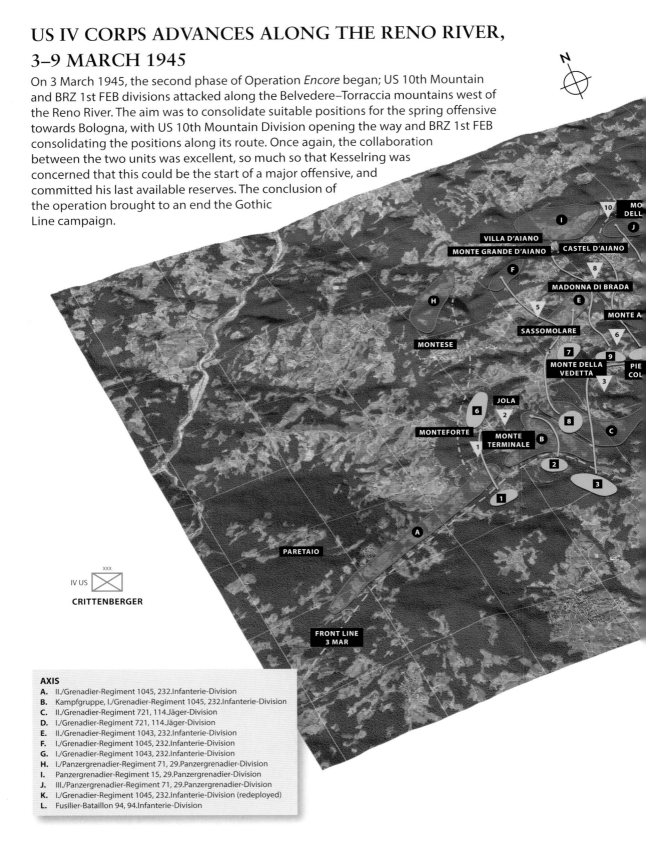

IV US $\boxed{\times\!\times\!\times}$

CRITTENBERGER

AXIS
- **A.** II./Grenadier-Regiment 1045, 232.Infanterie-Division
- **B.** Kampfgruppe, I./Grenadier-Regiment 1045, 232.Infanterie-Division
- **C.** II./Grenadier-Regiment 721, 114.Jäger-Division
- **D.** I./Grenadier-Regiment 721, 114.Jäger-Division
- **E.** II./Grenadier-Regiment 1043, 232.Infanterie-Division
- **F.** I./Grenadier-Regiment 1045, 232.Infanterie-Division
- **G.** I./Grenadier-Regiment 1043, 232.Infanterie-Division
- **H.** I./Panzergrenadier-Regiment 71, 29.Panzergrenadier-Division
- **I.** Panzergrenadier-Regiment 15, 29.Panzergrenadier-Division
- **J.** III./Panzergrenadier-Regiment 71, 29.Panzergrenadier-Division
- **K.** I./Grenadier-Regiment 1045, 232.Infanterie-Division (redeployed)
- **L.** Fusilier-Bataillon 94, 94.Infanterie-Division

Note: gridlines are shown at intervals of 2km (1.24 miles)

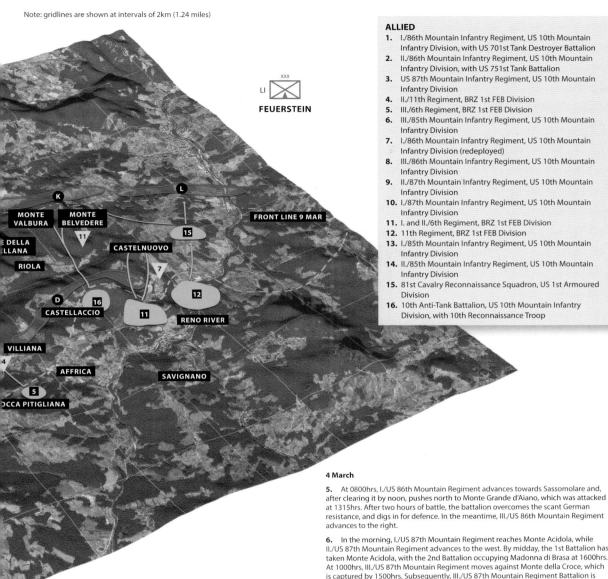

FEUERSTEIN

FRONT LINE 9 MAR

MONTE VALBURA

MONTE BELVEDERE

E DELLA LLANA

RIOLA

CASTELNUOVO

CASTELLACCIO

RENO RIVER

VILLIANA

AFFRICA

SAVIGNANO

OCCA PITIGLIANA

ALLIED

1. I./86th Mountain Infantry Regiment, US 10th Mountain Infantry Division, with US 701st Tank Destroyer Battalion
2. II./86th Mountain Infantry Regiment, US 10th Mountain Infantry Division, with US 751st Tank Battalion
3. US 87th Mountain Infantry Regiment, US 10th Mountain Infantry Division
4. II./11th Regiment, BRZ 1st FEB Division
5. III./6th Regiment, BRZ 1st FEB Division
6. III./85th Mountain Infantry Regiment, US 10th Mountain Infantry Division
7. I./86th Mountain Infantry Regiment, US 10th Mountain Infantry Division (redeployed)
8. III./86th Mountain Infantry Regiment, US 10th Mountain Infantry Division
9. II./87th Mountain Infantry Regiment, US 10th Mountain Infantry Division
10. I./87th Mountain Infantry Regiment, US 10th Mountain Infantry Division
11. I. and II./6th Regiment, BRZ 1st FEB Division
12. 11th Regiment, BRZ 1st FEB Division
13. I./85th Mountain Infantry Regiment, US 10th Mountain Infantry Division
14. II./85th Mountain Infantry Regiment, US 10th Mountain Infantry Division
15. 81st Cavalry Reconnaissance Squadron, US 1st Armoured Division
16. 10th Anti-Tank Battalion, US 10th Mountain Infantry Division, with 10th Reconnaissance Troop

▼ EVENTS

3 March

1. At 0800hrs, under intense artillery fire support, I./US 86th Mountain Regiment advances across the German defences and the minefields west of Monte Terminale, and are eventually relieved at 1100hrs by III./US 85th Mountain Infantry Regiment, which takes over the task of protecting the left flank of US 10th Mountain Infantry Division by setting up defensive positions to the west.

2. By 0840hrs, II./US 86th Mountain Infantry Regiment has overcome the German defences east of Monte Terminale, only to face stiff German resistance at Jola. With the support of US 701st Tank Destroyer Battalion, the village is seized by noon, resulting in the practical destruction of II./Grenadier-Bataillon 721, the commander of which is taken prisoner. The III./US 86th Mountain Regiment bypasses II./US 86th Mountain which is advancing towards Sassomolare.

3. US 87th Mountain Regiment, with its 3rd Battalion in the lead supported by US 751st Tank Battalion and air assets, enagages withdrawing German forces. The regiment seizes Monte della Vedetta, establishing a roadblock at Pietra Colora.

4. While BRZ II./11th Regiment advances along the flank of US 87th Mountain Regiment, BRZ III./6th Regiment secures the area around Rocca Pitigliana, clearing several hamlets as it goes.

4 March

5. At 0800hrs, I./US 86th Mountain Regiment advances towards Sassomolare and, after clearing it by noon, pushes north to Monte Grande d'Aiano, which was attacked at 1315hrs. After two hours of battle, the battalion overcomes the scant German resistance, and digs in for defence. In the meantime, III./US 86th Mountain Regiment advances to the right.

6. In the morning, I./US 87th Mountain Regiment reaches Monte Acidola, while II./US 87th Mountain Regiment advances to the west. By midday, the 1st Battalion has taken Monte Acidola, with the 2nd Battalion occupying Madonna di Brasa at 1600hrs. At 1000hrs, III./US 87th Mountain Regiment moves against Monte della Croce, which is captured by 1500hrs. Subsequently, III./US 87th Mountain Regiment Battalion is relieved by BRZ III./6th Regiment.

7. The BRZ I. and II./6th Regiment seize Castelnuovo by 1910hrs, while to the east BRZ 11th Regiment advances, covering the right flank.

5 March

8. With the seizure of Monte della Croce the final stage of the offensive is set, with I. and II./US 87th Mountain Regiment attacking Castel d'Aiano. I./US 87th Mountain Regiment captures the town, encountering elements from 29.Panzergrenadier-Division for the first time, while II./US 87th Mountain Regiment covers the left flank, establishing a continuous front with I. and III./US 86th Mountain Regiment.

9. At 0800hrs, the newly committed I. and II./US 85th Mountain Regiment begin their advance. The former secures Monte della Spe at 1800hrs, in spite of enemy resistance, the second takes Monte della Castellana at 1500hrs.

10. On the night of 5/6 March, elements from Panzergrenadier-Regiment 15 counter-attack Monte della Spe several times, but in spite of their efforts I./US 85th Mountain Regiment holds fast and remains on the summit.

6–9 March

11. Detached from US 1st Armored Division, on 6 March the US 81st Cavalry Reconnaissance Squadron moves ahead of BRZ 6th Regiment to create a continuous front with US 10th Mountain Division. On 9 March, US 10th Mountain Division's anti-tank battalion and reconnaissance troop seize Monte Valbura and Monte Belvedere, facing no opposition, before handing over the area to BRZ 1st FEB Division.

Men of the US 10th Mountain Division approaching a farm, March 1945. The division proved its worth during the end phase of the Gothic Line campaign, but too late to influence it decisively. (US Army)

With the arrival in January 1945 of US 86th Mountain Infantry Regiment, US 10th Mountain Division was now at full strength and deployed south-west of the Reno River valley, replacing US TF 45. This well-trained and well-equipped division only lacked heavy artillery, but along with BRZ 1st FEB it was selected for Operation *Encore*. The aim of the operation was to clear an area stretching over 16km west of the Reno and Route 64 from Pistoia to Bologna, in order to improve the starting positions for a spring 1945 offensive.

The operation began on 18 February in the freezing cold, with US 10th Mountain Division facing 232.Infanterie-Division, which was subsequently reinforced by 114. Jäger-Division. In spite of the poor weather and German counter-attacks, US 10th Mountain Division resumed its advance on 21 February, seizing Monte della Torraccia two days later, ending the first phase of the operation. The second phase, postponed because of the weather, began on 3 March with a swift American advance, which, two days later, faced the arrival of German reinforcements from 29.Panzergrenadier-Division. Generalfeldmarschall Kesselring, now back in command, was seriously concerned that this could be another drive to reach Bologna. The failure of the German counter-attacks enabled the US 10th Mountain Division to reach the area west of Vergato, while BRZ 1st FEB cleared the terrain from there to the Reno until Operation *Encore* was closed down on 10 March – US 10th Mountain Division having suffered 549 casualties. Less than a month later, the spring 1945 Allied offensive would lead to the end of the Italian campaign.

AFTERMATH

At first sight, the Gothic Line campaign appears similar to the Gustav Line campaign of 1943–44, except for the lack of notable key battles such as Cassino and Ortona, and for the fact that, as a goal, the Po River valley was no substitute for Rome. Understandably, the campaign has always suffered from the 'D-Day dodgers' complex. Issues such as the tying down of the German forces in Italy or the missed landing in Istria prevailed, and the value of the campaign itself has frequently been overlooked.

There are no accurate figures for losses, the only available data being that US Fifth Army lost some 21,500 American soldiers between 16 August and 15 December 1944. There are no details available on Brazilian, South African and BR XIII Corps losses, nor for BR Eighth Army losses overall, which can be estimated at about 27,000. German losses amounted to at least 73,500 between September and December 1944 in the entire theatre.

As such, the Gothic Line is accountable for about one-sixth of overall Allied losses, and one-third of German ones during the entire Italian campaign, which dispel the impression that it was a minor campaign, particularly when compared to simultaneous ones on the Western Front. It was a crucial campaign, as demonstrated by Hitler's determination to maintain control of northern Italy and by the Allied interest in its seizure, which was eventually achieved in spring 1945.

Unfortunately, the Allies failed to achieve their goal, namely breaking through the German defences and advancing towards Bologna and the Po River. The failure is even more remarkable if Allied superiority in terms of firepower and materiel, if not in manpower, is taken into account. Clearly, both the terrain and the enemy's capabilities were underestimated. Like in Operation *Market-Garden*, the Allied commanders persuaded themselves that only a last push was needed to make the German front crumble, which led to a series of mistakes. The Allied plan lacked focus and, given the manpower shortages, it should have required a concentrated effort on one single point. On the contrary, both the BR Eighth and the US Fifth armies carried out separate offensives (the latter dissipating its meagre resources even more), enabling the Germans to make fighting withdrawals from one defensive line to another, which allowed them to wear out the attacking forces and make it through to winter, effectively putting an end to the offensive.

This failure might have been avoided if US Fifth Army had attacked first, as the Germans expected, attracting enemy reserves to the area and making it possible for BR Eighth Army to drive through the Gothic Line defences and break through to Bologna and the Po. Instead, the Germans were able to deploy their reserves against BR Eighth Army first, while delaying the US Fifth Army offensive. General Clark's decision to divert US 88th Division to Imola surely contributed to the final failure of its offensive (which did not take into account limited American capabilities), along with the fact that when the focus shifted to US Fifth Army, BR Eighth Army's offensive in Romagna was already bogged down.

Above all, there was a clear issue among the Allied leadership. Apparently a victim of American dominance, British Field Marshall Alexander could or would not challenge US General Clark's ambitions to reach Bologna and the Po, and therefore planned a two-pronged offensive without the necessary resources. This enabled Kesselring and von Vietinghoff to shift units to wherever they were needed, in spite of the relentless Allied bombing of German rear areas, preventing any decisive breakthrough – resulting in the failure of the Allied offensive.

A Sherman-mounted T40/M17 'Whizbang' rocket launcher. Four tank battalions in Italy experimented with this weapon, including the 752nd, to which the tank shown here belonged. (PhotoQuest/Getty Images)

THE BATTLEFIELD TODAY

It would be a rather pointless exercise for those with an interest in the Gothic Line campaign to visit the coastal areas of Romagna, seeking traces of the campaign or individual battles. The entire stretch of coast from Ancona to Trieste has been developed as Italy's main tourist riviera, and it suffers from over-development and bears no trace of its former character. The situation is quite different inland, where, in spite of development and change, the terrain still bears traces of the war. The area of the rivers between the Rubicone (as Mussolini redesignated the former Fiumicino, after Caesar's well-known river) and the Senio today bears no resemblance to the 1944 battlefield. The riverbanks have been restored and evidence of earlier flood plains is lacking. Nevertheless, it is still possible to appreciate how the Germans could turn these rivers into impregnable defensive lines, which helped them to slow the Allied advance.

The Apennine mountains are even better from this point of view, since little has changed there and several German bunkers and defences have been preserved, if not even restored. Battlefield enthusiasts should avoid the modern Italian motorways and take the old roads in the same areas where the 1944 battles were fought. Here places like the Giogo Pass or Livergnano can be found; the latter, although completely rebuilt after the war, not only retains some resemblance to the old town, but also has a small Gothic Line campaign museum.

Since the Gothic Line campaign was fought in Italy's more developed northern regions, such as Emilia-Romagna and Tuscany, unlike other parts of the country several museums have been created at a local level, mostly with relics from the battlefields. The list of museums is quite impressive: Castel del Rio and Montese south of Bologna, Montegridolfo and Casinina west of Pesaro, the impressive museum of the battle for the Senio at Alfonsine, the Scarperia museum north of Florence, the Firenzuola museum and the Gothic Line museum near Pistoia. For a complete list of museums, their opening times and locations, it is advisable to check the internet.

For further information about interesting sites relating to the campaign, Italian-speaking readers are advised to consult these two interesting books: Gabriele Ronchetti's *La Linea Gotica: I Luoghi dell'Ultimo Fronte di Guerra in Italia* (published by Mattioli, 1985), and Antonio Melis' *La Linea Gotica: Guida ai Luoghi, alla Storia e ai Personaggi* (published by Editoriale Programma, 2019). Anne Leslie Saunders' *A Travel Guide to World War II Sites in Italy* (published by CreateSpace, 2010), although less detailed than the Italian-language offerings, is still an essential travel guide for anyone interested in the Italian theatre in World War II – particularly so, given the many useful insights needed by any foreign traveller visiting Italy.

FURTHER READING

Alexander, Harold, *The Alexander Memoirs* (London: Cassell, 1962)

Blackwell, Ian, *Fifth Army in Italy 1943–1945: A Coalition at War* (Barnsley: Pen & Sword, 2012)

Brooks, Thomas R., *The War North of Rome, June 1944–May 1945* (Edison, NJ: Castle Books, 2001)

Clark, Mark Wayne, *Calculated Risk* (New York, NY: Harper, 1950)

Delaney, Douglas E., *Corps Commanders: Five British and Canadian Generals at War* (Vancouver, Toronto: UBC Press, 2011)

Delaney, John P., *The Blue Devils in Italy: A History of the 88th Division in World War II* (Nashville, TN: Battery Press, 1988)

Doherty, Richard, *Eighth Army in Italy 1943–45: The Long Hard Slog* (Barnsley: Pen & Sword, 2007)

Fifth Army History. Part 7: The Gothic Line, Part 8: *The Second Winter* (Washington, DC: Historical Section, Headquarters Fifth Army, 1945)

Fisher, Ernest F. Jr, *Cassino to the Alps* (Washington, DC: US Army Center of Military History, 1993)

Jackson, General Sir William, *The Mediterranean and the Middle East*, Volume VI: *Victory in the Mediterranean* (London: HMSO, 1987–1988)

Jennings, Christian, *At War on the Gothic Line: Fighting in Italy 1944–45* (London and New York, NY: Macmillan, 2016)

Kay, Robin, *From Cassino to Trieste* (Wellington, New Zealand: Dept of Internal Affairs, Historical Publications Branch, 1967)

Kesselring, Albert, *Soldat bis zum letzten Tag* (Bonn, Germany: Athenäum, 1953)

Kriegstagebuch des Oberkommandos der Wehrmacht (Wehrmachtführungsstab), Volume IV (ed. Percy Ernst Schramm) (Bonn, Germany: Bernard & Graefe, 1961)

MacDonald, Charles B. and Mathews, Sidney T., *Three Battles: Arnaville, Altuzzo, and Schmidt* (Washington, DC: US Army Center of Military History, 1952)

Mallinson, Jennifer, *From Taranto to Trieste: Following the 2nd NZ Division's Italian Campaign, 1943–45* (Masterton, New Zealand: Fraser Books, 2019)

Nicholson, G.W.L., *The Canadians in Italy 1943–1945* (Ottawa, Canada: Queen's Printer and Controller of Stationery, 1956)

Orgill, Douglas, *The Gothic Line: The Italian Campaign Autumn 1944* (New York, NY: Modern Literary Editions, 1967)

Pal, Dharm, *The Campaign in Italy, 1943–45* (New Dehli, India: Combined Inter-Service Historical Section, 1960)

Pugsley, Christopher, *A Bloody Road Home: World War Two and New Zealand's Heroic Second Division* (Auckland, New Zealand: Penguin, 2014)

Zuhelke, Mark, *The Gothic Line: Canada's Month of Hell in World War II Italy* (Vancouver, Canada: Douglas & MacIntyre, 2003)

Zuhelke, Mark, *The River Battles: Canada's Final Campaign in World War II Italy* (Vancouver, Canada: Douglas & MacIntyre, 2019)

INDEX

Figures in **bold** refer to illustrations.